T0199147

## Also by the Author

Cook, Rosemarie S. (1990). *Counseling Families of Children with Disabilities.* Dallas: Word Publishing, 1990.

Cook, Rosemarie S. (1992). *Parenting a Child with Special Needs.* Grand Rapids, MI: Zondervan, 1992.

Hughes, Rosemarie Scotti, and Pamela C. Kloeppel. *SAIL: Self-Awareness in Language Arts: 108 Activities for Grades K-5.* Minneapolis: Educational Media Corporation, 1994.

# FOREVER
## *Parenting*

Voices of Parents of Adults with Special Needs

Rosemarie Scotti Hughes, Ph.D.

WESTBOW
PRESS®
A DIVISION OF THOMAS NELSON
& ZONDERVAN

WestBow Press books may be ordered through booksellers or by contacting:

WestBow Press
A Division of Thomas Nelson & Zondervan
1663 Liberty Drive
Bloomington, IN 47403
www.westbowpress.com
1 (866) 928-1240

ISBN: 978-1-9736-3854-4 (sc)
ISBN: 978-1-9736-3853-7 (e)

Library of Congress Control Number: 2018910357

Print information available on the last page.

WestBow Press rev. date: 10/25/2018

The introduction to this book is spot on! "Parenting is forever" is the truth; the experiences Dr. Hughes shares, personal and of others, offer insights, information and encouragement for that long-haul parenting job. The contents of this book tell a personal story, but also a common story. The lives mentioned in this book are hopeful yet raw, informed though constantly rediscovering, and by reading it you will be filled with new perspective.

Barbara J. Newman
Church and School Consultant, CLC Network

In weaving together this constellation of personal stories, Dr. Hughes shares a common journey that is rarely predictable but holds great rewards. For so many families impacted by disability, these stories will resonate and encourage. And for communities, these themes comprise an invitation to come alongside families in compelling ways that lead to flourishing.

Erik Carter
Cornelius Vanderbilt Professor of Special Education
Vanderbilt University, Nashville, TN

The grace and wisdom in *Forever Parenting* comes from honest and open interviews and portrayals of the lives of parents with adult children with various forms of disabilities. Rosemarie Hughes, as a parent herself, knows the questions to ask, teases out the lessons learned, and then weaves in her own experience in ways that do not pretend to say that one way of coping or parenting is better than another. She deliberately inquires about the role of faith in each of the family's stories, yet, again, does not presume to say that one kind of experience or belief is better than another. Thus, the best quality of the stories and book is that it feels very real, a non-pretentious resource in which families with adult children with disabilities will likely see parts of themselves, as well as learning from the caring commitment that each of the stories illustrates. As a reader, I felt like I was in the middle of a parent support group, where stories, not theories, give the members the ability to take from them what is most applicable and meaningful to their own lives. It can also help clergy and other helping professionals learn, and once again, realize that our role is to walk with families in their journeys rather than point them to destinations.

Bill Gaventa, M. Div.
Director, Summer Institute on Theology and Disability

Rosemarie Hughes' Forever *Parenting: Voices of Parents of Adults with Special Needs* is essential reading for parents and all those who are involved in their lives. Parenting changes as our children age and Rosemarie sensitively shares the unique and personal stories of families adapting to each new twist and turn of the journey. *Forever Parenting* gives readers the insider perspective as parents cope with individual challenges, struggles, surprises, and joys woven together by love and responsibility. As a parent of an adult child with a disability, I could relate my own family's journey and found a sense of comfort that I am not alone. I especially appreciate the candid interviews that these families gave and the genuine and authentic way Rosemarie writes about them. As a faith community disability inclusion professional, I was thrilled that Rosemarie raised the question about the role of God and faith on the journey.

Shelly Thomas Christensen
MA, DAAIDD

Author of *From Longing to Belonging: A Practical Guide to Including People with Disabilities in Your Faith Community*

*Forever Parenting* is a book that is real: Real stories expressing challenges and real solutions found by families. Parents of children with disabilities will find themselves in one or more of the stories if not now then at some time in the future. The lessons of these families will help in planning for the future for a reader's own child. *Forever Parenting* takes on the lament of the title. Parenting of children with disabilities continues on well into adulthood. But families have found joy and success through their faith. Readers will both weep with the stories and find strength through the parents who relate them. This book is filled with stories that are daunting and encouraging, unexpected and redeeming, frightful and wonderful. It is helpful for parents facing the challenges described and instructive for those who want to come alongside and provide loving support.

Jeff McNair, Ph.D.
Director, Church Relations - CID
Christian Institute on Disability
Joni and Friends International Policy Center

Rosemarie Hughes' *Forever Parenting* provides an intimate portrait of parenting children with disabilities. In the telling of her own story and those of others, she avoids the all-too-common inspirational sugar-coating and probes a depth of honesty in the hurt, challenge, and ultimate joy of this unique parenting experience. Her discussion questions and references invite the reader into a rich conversation about faith, families, and our walk together as people of God.

David Morstad
Larger Table Resources
Author of *Whole Community: Introducing Faith Communities to People with Intellectual and Developmental Disability*

Why are the parental voices gathered in this book so important? Because so many who care for adults with disabilities – not just parents but siblings, relatives, and friends – feel they are so alone and do not have others to share the journey with. *Forever Parenting* thus brings together over a dozen voices that become guides for these difficult segments of life's journey while also providing or pointing the way to many other social, governmental, and ecclesial resources to undergird and expand the care of our loved ones as they grow older. For any who wonder not just how to survive but to thrive as caretakers of adults with challenging needs, Rosemarie Hughes is an indispensable and invaluable coach.

Amos Yong, author of *The Bible, Disability & the Church*
Professor of Theology and Mission, Fuller University Seminary, Pasadena, CA

Through personal experience and thorough interviews with dozens of parents of adult children with disabilities, Dr. Hughes paints an honest yet encouraging picture of the joys and challenges of this unique parenting journey. As the parent of a young adult who has autism, I was captivated by the stories in *Forever Parenting*, curious to learn what other parents experience as their children with special needs approach adulthood. As the Executive Director of Faith Inclusion Network, I am thrilled to be able to recommend *Forever Parenting* to faith communities, parents, and disability service providers as a book that takes readers beyond the childhood years and contributes to a greater awareness and understanding of individuals and families affected by disability.

Karen Jackson
Executive Director, Faith Inclusion Network of Hampton Roads
Author, *Loving Samantha*

# DEDICATION

To my parents, Louis Anthony Scotti and Carmela LaRocca Scotti, who always believed in me, encouraged me, and most of all, loved me. Dad died at age forty-five, when I was thirteen, but I never forgot his inspiration to reach for the higher ground. Mom, who died in 2003 at age ninety, was my lifelong supporter and cherished all her grandsons; she was a model for me by meeting life head-on and carrying on, no matter what.

# ACKNOWLEDGMENTS

Thank you to all of the parents who so graciously gave of their time for interviews. I send a ginormous thank you to Dianne Pruden, friend, lunch buddy, fellow connoisseur of clip earrings, and most importantly volunteer first editor. To D. Michael Geller, MD, MSW, of Broader Focus, LLC, thank you for the courtesy of the cover photo that is a part of telling my story.

# INTRODUCTION

This book is for those unheralded and mostly unacknowledged heroes, parents of adults with special needs. In my previous books I wrote about families who had children under twenty-one years old with disabilities. I was diagnosed with cancer recently, which gave me a sense of urgency to complete this project. I underwent surgery and am cancer-free at this time. I pray I remain so. However, I am much more aware of how days and months can easily slip by with unmet goals, and so this work became a priority for me.

When my son Chris was younger, I naively thought that once I had him settled into a good residential and work placement, I would have some time off from being his active-duty mom. However, events proved me wrong, and it seemed I always had a new battle to fight on a new front. Dealing with the demands of having an adult with special needs was a new world, since adults are without the protective elements of prescriptive laws for education. The quest to obtain needed services for our children changes substantially once the school bus stops coming. There are no more mandated services, and parents are often on their own to seek out the best situations for housing, working, recreating, and socializing. Families naturally change over time. In a normal progression of family life, parental relationships with children usually adjust from direct parenting to supportive and encouraging roles as adult children mature and sometimes have their own families. Parents of adults with special needs may see progress at a very slow rate, if at all, and often must remain in a direct parenting role despite their own concerns with work, health, retiring, or aging. When you are a parent of a special needs child, parenting is forever.

I wrote this book to give parents and other caregivers encouragement, let them know they're not alone, and give those who are not involved with the special needs community an awareness of the concerns of these families. I also wanted to tell the stories of courage, determination, love, faith, and hope that kept these families focused on their child's needs, and how they overcame adversity and kept moving forward. None of the parents in this book are perfect, myself included, but they all did the best they could under the circumstances, and all continue to try to be the best they can be as parents. None of us volunteered to have a child with special needs, yet all of us continued keeping on, day after day, in our caring. There is no magic formula for balancing this responsibility with the rest of our family, career, and self-care needs except to dig in and do it.

Many books about parenting adults with special needs focus on laws, regulations, finding services, and financial arrangements. These topics are all valid, but I chose to focus mainly on the realities of daily living to show parental struggles, decisions, and family dynamics. It is in the trenches that real life occurs, and parents of special needs adults, advocates, and caregivers can benefit from the experiences of these families. Every individual story was unique, and yet all of the stories had common elements. Each family had a different story and a different path, but all those I interviewed wanted the same thing: the best possible life for their loved one.

I limited my research in this book to families who had adult children who were identified as having intellectual or developmental disabilities before they were age eighteen and are now over that age. As our children with special needs age, we have less regular contact with other parents in the same situation. When Chris was young and in school, I had regular interaction with other parents, primarily at school programs. It was the one place I didn't feel like the only one out there with a child with special needs. Sadly, that regular parental contact ended when his schooling ended. Many families with adults with disabilities are without a touchpoint such as school; I hope this book serves as a sense of affinity for them.

It was a privilege to interview the people in this book, and I am sincerely grateful to each one. My hope is that these stories will provide information and help caregivers, advocates, and the public realize the many considerations involved in parenting adults with special needs. Laws, regulations, and policies are often enacted without full realization of the true consequences for those people with special needs who are being regulated.

These stories are a small sampling of the large numbers of families with adult children with disabilities. However, you can find variations of the same stories in any community. Common themes emerged from the stories, even though each family's situation was different. Some of those themes included the following:

- Many children were not diagnosed correctly for several months or years (in one case, only after death).
- Families met obstacles in finding the best school, day support, and employment.
- Faith was a major part of most parents' coping abilities.
- Almost all of the parents were concerned about care for their child after they themselves died.
- Most parents felt that their job was one of constant advocacy and oversight.
- Not all parents know the best resources in their community for future planning.
- Parents recognized their ongoing caregiving depleted their energy and damaged their health.
- Many parents went forward to fill gaps in the system, such as founding schools, establishing support groups, developing assistance associations, or contributing to these types of organizations.
- All parents mentioned the problems involved with their child but also talked about the gifts they brought to the family.
- Parents ignored the advice of doctors who told them to institutionalize their children and forget about them.
- All parents were proud of how far their children had come.
- Many parents felt that their family members had gained compassion through their experience.

These themes provided reasons for parents to continue to seek out the best and not settle for just good enough. Even when weary of the effort, parents continued to find services that fit the child and not the reverse. These parents were not afraid to be the squeaky wheel when necessary but also learned the essential art of communicating effectively with the caregivers and service providers in their child's life.

Parents of children with special needs are strong, stronger than they realize, even when their problems seem unsolvable. Strength can come from taking time to cherish the good, appreciate the happy, and celebrate small gains. I can still remember the day about thirty-five years ago when I was overjoyed after Chris had finally learned to tie his own shoelaces. This major development was due to the efforts of Kathy, a friend who needed a project for a university class. Although Kathy passed on a few years ago, I never look at Chris's shoelaces without thinking of (and thanking) her.

My own family now includes an infant grandson with a dynamite personality who has partial hearing loss and a grandson and step-grandson with attention-deficit hyperactivity disorder (ADHD), who are both clever, kind, and engaging children. Although I will probably not be around for the majority of their life journeys, I support their parents, although separated by many miles, as much as I can.

I firmly believe that God is all about economy, with none of our life experiences going to waste. I have often found unintended positive results when I least expected them. Parents of children with disabilities have a special bond. As you read my words, you become a welcome part of my ever-expanding community. I extend to you two of my favorite verses from the Bible. The first is part of John 10:10, and one that I pray constantly for Chris: "I am come that they might have life, and that they might have it more abundantly." The second is Isaiah 54:13, a verse that I pray daily for all of my family: "And all thy children shall be taught of the LORD; and great shall be the peace of thy children."

My ultimate desire for this book is that with awareness will come understanding, and with understanding, support for those who are forever parenting.

The stories in this book are derived from my interviewing people and taking notes during the interview. I have tried to present as accurately as possible the content of the interviews. I obtained permission to use names in those chapters where actual names are given. The ages and circumstances of people portrayed in the chapters of this book were those at the time of the interview.

## CHAPTER 1

# *Celebrating Christopher*

Christopher Guy Cook, better known as Chris, is my adult son; he has an intellectual disability. He was the impetus for my enrolling in graduate school, albeit with trepidation, seventeen years after earning my bachelor's degree. After navigating through many systems and meetings over the years, I wanted to help other parents who had children with special needs. I can also thank him for the renewal of my spiritual life when he was ten years old and I was at the end of my rope, with no more room to tie knots and hang on. I credit him with being the stimulus that pushed me to write books and articles, and participate in conferences and organizations where I met so many wonderful people with similar concerns for people with disabilities.

There were many years when I did not celebrate having Christopher as a son. Raising him and his three brothers was a tremendously difficult job. The problem was not with my children, but with the circumstances. The four boys, with nine years between oldest and youngest, were (and still are) loving, kind, and enjoyable persons. They were also very active boys. When the children were young, we were a Navy family, moving from coast to coast: Atlantic to Pacific to Gulf of Mexico and back to Atlantic. The closest we ever lived to our families was 450 miles. Having a child with special needs, plus three others, and a father who was often on deployment was a stressful, but never dull, life.

In *Parenting the Child with Special Needs* (1992), I included the story of our family life for Chris's first twenty-one years. I described the joy of Chris as a newborn, desperately trying to cope with Chris as a child, and celebrating him as an adult. It has been an unpredictable and life-changing journey.(1)

The parents I interviewed for this book went through myriad medical professionals to obtain an accurate diagnosis, proper treatment, and programs for their children who had problems either at birth or shortly afterward. My story is similar. Despite noticing significant developmental delays in Chris, I did not get affirmation from doctors that he had a disability until he was three years old. That process involved military and civilian doctors in three states.

When he was three, Chris was diagnosed as having a disability; our family was traveling by car on permanent change of station orders, with a planned stopover in Pittsburgh to be with family. When we arrived in Pittsburgh, Chris's knee was infected, and we took him to a hospital emergency room, where he was treated for an insect bite. However, the knee looked worse a few days later, and we took him to a local doctor, who diagnosed impetigo. The doctor also told us that by her observation, Chris was acting more like an eighteen-month-old child rather than a three-year-old and referred us to testing at a local hospital, which we did. We arrived at our new duty station with a diagnosis of severe intellectual impairment, still reeling from that label and trying to process what it meant for our family.

After we settled in our new home, I struggled to find programs for help. At that time, there was no military Special Needs Family Members program, no Navy Fleet and Family Services, no public preschool for a three-year-old with special needs, and no Medicaid waivers for help. Eventually, I found a local nonprofit agency, and through them, Chris attended a private half-day program in a church for a year, then an early intervention half-day program sponsored by the city, and then a private full-time day program. Through testing in those settings, he acquired some new diagnoses, such as learning disabled and possible schizophrenia, neither of which proved to be accurate. It was humorous and a credit to Chris's talents that one doctor referred to him as "the child with a limp," as he was perfectly mimicking his classmate who had cerebral palsy.

My third son was born when Chris was four, and that became a tipping point for me. Dad was on sea duty, and Chris became jealous of his new brother. I was surprised because Chris was a sweet child and loved his older brother. I would often have to nurse the baby with Chris perched on my knee so I could read a book to him to give him the attention he wanted. However, as the new baby became a toddler, Chris constantly sought my attention even more. Life was chaotic, mainly because I was trying to meet the little one's needs while giving Chris what he needed. Although I had a degree in elementary education and teaching experience, I did not have the wisdom or resources to meet the many needs of a largely nonverbal child while taking care of his five-year-old brother and a baby. Over the next three years, I looked for options. Through one program, a behavioral specialist came to our home and gave me a golf counter to record stressful incidents and then report these back to him. I was clicking that golf counter so many times that after a few days, I quit the program and resumed taking care of the children the best I knew how. I did not feel I had the luxury of observation while turmoil erupted all around. I next went to a military pediatrician to seek help. After more testing, he recommended placing Chris in an out-of-state school, as we had exhausted all local resources.

A private school was expensive and beyond our budget, but at that time the military and the city each contributed enough to pay for tuition. Chris was in a residential private school out of state from age seven to nine. I recently reread his reports from that time, and they reflect the caring and professional climate of the school. The staff taught him many basic living skills and met his needs. However, his being away, while bringing respite, was difficult for the family. It was especially distressing for me to send off a seven-year-old who could not understand what was happening, and I shed many tears, but I felt I had no alternative. We traveled five hundred miles round trip to spend a weekend with him or to bring him home for holidays and summer vacations. My fourth child was born during this time, and at one point Mom, Dad, and three kids shared a hotel room to visit Chris. Funding for that schooling ended when Chris was nine, and from age nine to twenty-two, he was in the local public school system in self-contained special needs classes.

When Chris completed school at age twenty-two, I needed to find a place for him because his father and I both worked full time. There were no Medicaid waiver caregiving services to facilitate remaining in the home at that time. Making the initial decision not to keep Chris at home was once again heartbreaking. However, I knew that once school was over, the potential for a day program or job for him was limited because due to work schedules, we could not provide the transportation he would need. In a residential situation, the transportation and placement would be provided. Also, I knew that Chris needed to learn more social, work, and self-care skills. Parents do not live forever, and aging often brings health problems. Having to find emergency caregivers or an emergency placement in case of death or disability of parents would be the worst possible scenario for Chris. Not only would he lose a parent, he'd also lose his home and routine. I did not want that kind of crisis for him, ever.

His father and I decided to enroll him to live and work in a program that was about sixty miles away. My sadness was the same as when I prepared him to leave home when he was seven, and I again cried daily as I sewed labels on his clothes. Although I did not feel it was the optimal place for him, because it was so large, it was the best I could find at the time and it was close enough to bring him home for weekends and holidays. Unfortunately, during Chris's time there my marriage ended. Because this was a stressful and uncertain time, it was a blessing to have Chris settled, even if not optimal, while we went through with selling our home, moving, and the divorce. I also had to search for a new place to live for me and two of his brothers, as the oldest was married by then. God was gracious and provided a buyer before I even put a "For Sale" sign up in the yard. I also found a townhome to rent in our school district on a recommendation from a friend on a Saturday, literally meeting the agent on Sunday morning as the former tenants were moving out.

Four years after Chris's initial adult placement ended, a space opened in a local group home, and from that time, he has been under the care of the same organization. Last year, the twelve-person group home he was in closed, and smaller homes were opened. Chris moved to a four-person home twenty-five minutes from me, and I feel that this is the best situation he has ever been in. He enjoys his large bedroom and bath, he has an outdoor basketball hoop, and in the garage are an indoor basketball game and game machines. He attends a day support/work program during the week and enjoys many social events, Special Olympics, and a bowling league. About once a month, he stays overnight at my home on a weekend, and we go to church together, especially on holidays. We also eat out, which is one of his favorite activities. Chris loves to fly with me on our annual Christmas trips to Atlanta to visit with his youngest brother and his family. He also attends a summer camp annually and spends some holidays and vacations with his father.

However, even though I have faith in God's provision, I never take for granted that Chris's situations will be static. Recently, Medicaid waivers and some regulations changed, and the work placement he had for twenty-five years changed to offer day support only. It took about five months to find a new placement that offers a combination of work and day support. The work element was important, as Chris is proud of what he accomplishes. He is doing well and enjoys this new venture. I am grateful that things worked out so well and very aware that this was a blessing.

Currently, I am the only family member who lives near Chris; all others are 150 miles or more away. In 1992, I remarried, and Chris gained Roger as a stepfather, who was a great help to me with Chris. However, he died in 2012 and left a vacuum both for me and Chris in many ways. As much as I can, I've put provisions in place for Chris in the event of my death. It would fall to his brothers and his father (if he outlives me) to become the main people who, in cooperation with his caregivers, would attend to Chris.

Providing what is best for Chris as an adult is a repeat of trying to find suitable situations for him as a child, but with more factors to consider. As a parent, I find myself taking on many roles, some easier than others. I call it "being in the school of Christopher," and that is where I probably earned my first graduate degree. Although not complete, the following is a list of some of the areas that parents of children with disabilities have to learn:

- behavior management
- nutrition
- medical coordination and management
- laws and regulations of their state
- federal laws
- local resources

- financial planning
- school law
- coordination of services
- transportation
- interfacing with local, state, and federal agencies
- communication with caregivers
- hiring caregivers
- advocacy skills
- balancing family life
- self-care
- future planning

As a parent, a constant focus on the special needs person can consume an individual or a family. A couple can become stronger through working together, but they may also grow apart for many reasons. I researched several databases and blogs to find rates of divorce and separation when there is a child with special needs in the family but could not find a definitive answer.

The usually stated overall divorce rate of 50 percent in the United States is deceptive because that statistic is for all new marriages and remarriages. It doesn't mean that half of everyone marrying for the first time will divorce. I found blogs and popular articles that supported a divorce rate of 80 percent when there is a special needs child in the family, but that is a fabricated statistic, produced from speculation. There is no data that provides an accurate number. However, it is safe to say that the higher the stress in the family, the more likelihood of divorce. Research studies demonstrate what produces the most stress in families with a special needs child. One study looked at effects of child disability on the family and noted the financial strain from health care and other specialized services that are needed.(2)

Added to that burden was the difficulty for parents to find appropriate childcare, which may result in fewer hours available for work, particularly for mothers. The nature of the disability played a crucial factor in the level of stress in the family. Parents of children with Down syndrome or with intellectual disability had lower levels of stress than those whose children were autistic or had emotional disabilities. The subjects in this study were measured over three points in the child's life, from ages six through seventeen. The authors of the paper noted that they could not reach a conclusion about the long- term effect on families. They were unable to determine whether burdens increased on the families or if the families learned to cope.

A 2015 paper published in *The Exceptional Parent* presented a multitude of factors that influenced the rate of divorce among families with a child with Down syndrome. The authors noted the "two-parent arc," which is a geographical picture of where children are more likely to be living with both parents in the United States, as opposed to having parents who did not marry or who were divorced. This arc begins in Utah, travels through North and South Dakota and Minnesota, and then goes to New England and New Jersey. Single parents are more likely to be found in Nevada, New Mexico, Oklahoma, and the Deep South and continue through Appalachia and West Virginia. Education rates of parents and young ages at marriage in these states are a significant factor in high divorce rates. What is important to the individual family is not the gathered data, but the significance of the divorce to the child with special needs and a plan for the best of care for that child.(3)

A 2014 study of Air Force families with special needs children focused on resiliency. The goal of the study was to identify those factors that would help the family stay together through the stress of having a child with a disability. The results were that the stronger the support systems, the more resilient the family and the more able to cope with challenges. Those support systems were the spouse and the extended family, and then community, military, and other social supports.(4)

In my counseling practice, I operated on the theory that a marriage is dead long before the divorce. The marriage dies, and the divorce is the funeral. As my own marital separation and subsequent divorce happened after twenty-five years of marriage, I can identify a number of events that combined to erode our relationship over those years. I cannot say that Chris was the single cause, but to be totally honest, he was one of the stress points, through no fault of his own. I can only speculate that perhaps there would have been no divorce, with a long list of "ifs." If we had fewer miles between us and our own parents so that we could have had more support, or if there were fewer Navy deployments, or if we did not have to move so often, or if we had fewer children, or if there were fewer battles to fight to get Chris services, but I will never know.

At this point in Chris's life, the past is mostly irrelevant, and only his present and future are worthy of focus as to his well-being. I do all I can, and I will admit that some days, I feel guilty that it's not enough, whatever "it" is. I have no crystal ball and must deal with Chris's needs day by day as they arise or circumstances change. One day, Chris's brothers will take over those duties. It will never be the same as Mom, but that doesn't mean that different will not be good for Chris. I gave my sons the best parenting I knew how to give at the time, and I see what great parents they are to their own children. Most days, I have a peace that when the time comes, all will be well. Those other days, when doubts and fears overwhelm me, I turn back to a promise from many years ago (not audible, but a sense that God was talking to me) that God loves Chris even more than I do, and that He will care for this beloved child. I have to rely on my faith in that promise.

# Questions for Discussion or Self-Reflection

1. Chris has had several significant points that were crucial in his life. What are those markers in your child's life?

_____

_____

_____

_____

_____

_____

2. At the time when Chris was growing up, parents had limited information about their child's condition and needs. What tools do you find most helpful now in learning about your child's needs?

_____

_____

_____

_____

_____

_____

3. How can parents divide time among all the children in the family so they don't feel that their sibling with a disability gets most of the parents' attention?

_____

_____

_____

_____

_____

_____

4. How often do all the members of your family communicate about the present and future needs of your child? How effective is this communication?

_____

_____

_____

_____

_____

5. Who is the keeper of the information about your child with special needs? Who makes important decisions? What is your approach to problem solving?

_____

_____

_____

_____

_____

## CHAPTER 2

# Parenting without a GPS

*Marsha and Robert are fictitious names.*

When a parent and newborn meet for the first time, the journey begins. However, there are no maps to guide you, and no one knows the final destination. We often learn parenting step-by-step as our children grow, even though we have some guidelines as to what to expect at certain ages. I've often told my first son that I practiced parenting on him. When a child has special needs, the usual developmental guidelines are of little help, except to show what's not happening on the ideal timeline.

As children with special needs become adults, the goals of the school-based Individualized Educational Plan (IEP) no longer apply. New planning begins. On paper, the goal is to fit a program to an individual. Many states use the Supports Intensity Scale (SIS) or a similar assessment to determine what supports a person needs.(1) The SIS includes all aspects of a person's life, but services are not always available. The reality is that the person usually has to fit into supports available, rather than having supports fit the person. Programs are often limited to what the staff can provide or to restrictions in laws, rather than a primary focus on what the person needs or wants. The state where the person with special needs lives also determines what is available.

After my husband, Roger, died, I considered moving to Georgia to be closer to some of my family, but I did not want to leave Chris living in another state. When I called agencies in Georgia to find out what was available, I was told that they were still finding community placements for those currently in institutions; Chris would be placed on the bottom of the list for services, which would then probably take two to three years to be realized. In addition, Medicaid waivers do not travel state to state; he would be on the bottom of the list to get a new waiver. Medicaid waivers are important for more than medical expenses. They fund day programs, transportation, and residential living. It hardly seems fair that you are placed on a waiting list because you wish to relocate. People with disabilities are not free to live where they or their families wish, unless they are financially self-supporting.(2)

## Marsha and Robert

Marsha's story about her twenty-eight-year-old son, Robert, and his journey from living with his father in one state to living with her in another state took several unpredictable twists and turns. Marsha and Robert's father are divorced. Robert is the middle child, with an older brother who is thirty-one and younger sister, twenty-three. His brother is married with three children and lives about sixty miles from Marsha, and his sister is married and lives near his father. At our first interview, Marsha felt as though she were in limbo because of what she called her "twenty-eight-year-long struggle." Her frustration clearly showed when she stated, "There's no manual for these kids." At that point, she didn't know how to obtain services for Robert. There was no destination for her GPS to find.

Robert had a normal birth, but by the time he was three years old, Marsha noticed speech problems, which required speech therapy throughout most of his school years. In physical education classes, he could not run. He was also diagnosed with attention-deficit hyperactivity disorder (ADHD), but the medications flattened his affect so much that Marsha stated he was "like a zombie." Currently, Robert cannot read or write beyond a fourth grade level. However, he is skilled in manual dexterity; Marsha said he could fix a lawn mower motor when he was eight.

Robert first attended a school in his home state, where he was placed in self-contained special education classes with children who were at a lower developmental level than him. He began imitating his classmates' behaviors, such as biting people and pulling his hair. He subsequently was moved to smaller classes with children who were closer to his ability level. He had various assistants throughout his schooling, but the quality varied. In fourth and fifth grades, the assistants did all the work for him, according to Marsha. In high school, he was included in regular classes and only survived because of his assistant.

Over the course of his life, Robert was labeled learning disabled and then mildly intellectually impaired; he is now diagnosed as intellectually disabled. Six years ago, he went to a foot doctor who diagnosed him with cerebral palsy, which was the first time this disorder was mentioned to Marsha. He later had successful surgery to cut the Achilles tendons and break and reset the bones in his feet, which alleviated his constant pain.

Marsha's main concern for Robert is his vulnerability. He cannot discern who he can safely talk to or invite to visit when Marsha is not at home. She's also worried someone could give him drugs or entice him to go off with them. In 2014, he spent one year at a rehabilitation facility to learn working skills. After that, he sometimes lived with his brother; while he did generally obey the family rules, it was stressful for that family. On one occasion, he tried to travel by bus to meet a girl he met online. Fortunately, his brother caught up with him in time to stop his trip.

Robert still has some speech problems. He wants to drive, but Marsha will not allow it for many reasons. He cannot take the bus to a job or program because he can easily get lost and cannot remember his mother's address. He has no concept of the value of money. Marsha was under stress every day worrying about Robert. She stated that she was a strong person and that prayer got her through each day.

I interviewed Marsha for a second time four months later. In an attempt to obtain services for Robert in the local community, she had to dissuade a psychologist who argued against giving Robert any kind of a diagnosis. After she related the results of the testing when he was sixteen and explained the extent of his disabilities, the psychologist finally wrote up the diagnosis. As a result, Robert received services through the Department for Aging and Rehabilitative Services (DARS), which is a federal/state agency.(3)

Recently, Robert had an assistant for fifteen hours a week, which

Marsha said made all the difference in the world. The assistant came to the house three days a week and worked on basic life skills and social skills with Robert. He took him bowling; Robert enjoyed his new companion and activities. Unfortunately, the assistant's attendance became sporadic, and Marsha had to look for a new resource.

As a result, Robert is now living in an apartment supervised by a nonprofit agency. He has a job coach and may soon get a part-time position detailing cars. Marsha felt confident about the organization and was excited about this new turn in Robert's life.

Marsha works in financial planning. She recently related to me that she believes God is guiding her to help others with the same types of struggles she's had and is excited about the prospects of doing so. For example, at her workplace, she was able to assist an elderly couple who had a fifty-eight-year-old son with special needs who was still living at home. They had never applied to receive Social Security Income (SSI) for him. She is helping them with future planning for their son. Marsha feels that their office will be helping more aging parents who have children with special needs.

As Marsha and I and so many other parents have realized, there's often a wide gap between what we want for our adult child with special needs and what's available. I recently completed an online survey on Family and Individual Needs for Disability Supports (FINDS) through the ARC and Research and Training Center on Community Living at the University of Minnesota.(4) One of the questions was about what I considered to be the ideal living situation for the person with a disability in my family. I had to ponder this question because I've never thought about what was ideal. I've always had to settle for what was available. There were several choices for a response to this question: living in his own home that he rents or owns, living like a family member in another's home, living with a sibling, living in a group home, living in an institution, or living home with me. The one response that caught my attention and caused some reflection was "in an apartment building or intentional community living situation that includes both people with disabilities and those without."

An intentional community is one that is planned and designed for shared values to exist in a cooperative framework. There are traditional models such as a monastery, kibbutzim, or commune, and there are also newer models such as housing cooperatives and ecovillages. Jean Vanier's L'Arche movement is an example of such a situation, although in the United States, the model is of small group homes in neighborhoods, rather than in villages. Vanier stated, "The secret of L'Arche is relationship: meeting people, not through the filters of certitudes, ideologies, idealism or judgments, but heart to heart; listening to people with their pain, their joy, their hope, their history, listening to their heart beats."(5)

An intentional community moves away from the model of paid caregivers and also allows residents to choose roommates. The person's needs dictate daily life rather than having to choose from a menu of program offerings into which you have to fit. New regulations for Medicaid waivers encourage community integration and discourage the isolation of past models. The regulations could perhaps support ecovillages, much like Vanier's original concept, where people with and without disabilities live together. Medicaid is authorized by the federal government, but each state has its own regulations and administration. However, at this time, it's uncertain whether Medicaid would support the ecovillage concept. This concept is another area for parents to band together to demand legislative changes to best accommodate their children with special needs.

I honestly don't know what the ideal situation for Chris would be because it requires some forecasting based on dreams and wishes, rather than what may actually be best for him at a given period in his life. I have to exercise my faith in God's loving providence and provision for his future. I operate on a mix of advocacy and faith, as I suspect other parents of adults with disabilities do.

# Questions for Discussion or Self-Reflection

1. Marsha faced a lot of obstacles in finding needed services for Robert. What kind of obstacles have you faced?

_____

_____

_____

_____

_____

2. Do you consider such obstacles are a dead-end or a challenge to find another way to solve a problem?

_____

_____

_____

_____

_____

3. What resources can parents utilize when facing a seemingly hopeless situation?

_____

_____

_____

_____

_____

4. What do you envision is the best long-term living situation for your child with special needs?

_____

_____

_____

_____

_____

5. Have you ever had a family meeting to discuss the next steps for the person in your family with a disability? If yes, how was that productive? If no, this could be a possibility for your family. What would it take to make it happen?

_____

_____

_____

_____

_____

6. If there are siblings, what have they told you about their desire to be an active person in their sibling's life? How has this affected your planning?

_____

_____

_____

_____

_____

## CHAPTER 3

# The Mother-Daughter Book Club

*All names in this chapter are fictional.*

Most people are familiar with the concept of a book club: A group of people decide to read the same novel and then meet for a discussion. I was honored to be invited to attend a unique book club at a group home village, two separate homes for twenty-four men and women who were multidisabled. The residents, all in wheelchairs, are adults who are totally reliant upon their caregivers for the functions of daily living. The Mother-Daughter Book Club has met every Sunday afternoon for four years at this group home, which is an intermediate care facility (ICF).

Unlike most book clubs, only half of the participants can read and speak—the moms. Each mother takes turns reading from the selected book. Occasionally, the reading stops and the women discuss characters or plots from past chapters. This book club progresses at a slow rate because it only covers each week what can be read aloud in about an hour or so and so stopping for review is necessary.

I felt privileged to attend and participate in the club one Sunday afternoon. When I was not reading aloud, I was observing the interactions of the mothers and daughters. I noticed that each mom, when she wasn't reading, was making sure her daughter was comfortable, that her clothing was smoothed out, that she had a sip of a drink if needed, and generally giving many caring touches. The daughters were, for the most part, without expression, as they had little capacity to exhibit emotion. Even with the lack of expression by the daughters, I had a strong sense of the loving bonds in these pairs and was humbled by these young women whose minds were trapped in their bodies. My emotions were strong that day, as my own son is physically healthy, strong, and totally mobile, and I was viewing a very different side of the disability spectrum. I also saw the positive social support network these moms were for each other.

## Barb and Cathy

Barb is a widow, and her daughter, Cathy, is forty-nine years old. Cathy was born with a genetic disorder, a deletion of one of the arms of an X chromosome, which resulted in multiple problems. Although she is nonverbal, Cathy understands what is happening around her and conveys her likes and dislikes. Barb showed me Cathy's beautifully decorated room with seaside themed colors and fabrics chosen by Cathy with the help of a decorator. Barb was married to a career naval officer, Ray, who died of cancer in 2007, six years after his diagnosis. Cathy has two brothers, aged forty-seven and forty-five, one of whom has always been especially protective of Cathy.

Cathy was born in a military hospital in the southern United States that had no air conditioning; Barb described it as a "concentration camp." In addition to the dismal physical surroundings, the attitude of her caregivers was also disheartening. A doctor told her, "No one can ever say she was a pretty baby," which was hurtful and discouraging. Cathy had cleft lip surgery when she was three months old. At age six months, multiple issues emerged, and there were many trips to the emergency room: her hips were tight, she had pneumonia, she slept a lot, she had grand mal seizures, and she had coughing spells. A spinal tap was performed, and the diagnosis was that Cathy had no corpus callosum in her brain. The corpus callosum is a band of nerve fibers that connects the right and left hemispheres of the cerebrum. The doctors advised Barb to put Cathy into an institution and forget about her. Barb ignored that advice, and she and Ray cared for Cathy in their home. They sent her to a public school with self-contained special education classes until age twenty-two and then had her at home with a daytime caregiver for many years. She participated in a day support program before moving into her current residence.

Barb's sons were initially against any placement outside of the home for Cathy, but after Ray's death, Cathy became too much for Barb to care for on a daily basis, and placing her nearby was a good solution. Barb regularly takes Cathy out to hockey games and theatrical plays, but she's concerned about being able to continue doing so. Cathy has gained some weight, and it's now difficult for Barb to lift her in and out of the wheelchair. Barb felt that staff should be able to control her weight by watching her diet. Barb would like to see Cathy in a smaller group home. She said that with eleven other residents to care for, it's hard for staff to individualize care.

"One size does not fit all," she stated.

Barb is a Roman Catholic and sees Cathy as "a blessing and an inspiration." She related a spiritual experience she had that led her to believe that Cathy would die before she herself did; she no longer worried about what might happen when she was no longer alive to care for her. Barb prefaced her statement by saying that she is not one of those people who are "at one with the universe," which I took to mean a New-Ager, but she was sure the experience was of God. She was looking in the mirror one day and heard, not audibly, but in her spirit, God telling her that Cathy would die first. She carries that assurance with her, and it comforts her.

During the interview, we discussed military benefits, and I gave her information about new rules regarding the Survivors Benefits Plan and trusts for Cathy that could influence her financial future in a positive manner. I did not expect to be a source of information to parents as I conducted these interviews, but that is what evolved, and I also received information: an unexpected positive benefit of the interview process.

## Doris and Susan

Doris is the other mom from the Mother-Daughter Book Club I interviewed. Her daughter, Susan, is thirty-four. She is medically stable overall, but like Cathy, she is nonverbal and has no control over her limbs. Susan and her husband, Harry, live in a second-floor condo, and although they have an elevator, they can no longer bring Susan to their home for a visit. Because she is in her wheelchair, Susan cannot fit into the elevator because of the way she throws herself back, and they cannot carry her up the steps. Doris has back problems, which makes tending to her daughter's needs impossible, so Doris and Harry visit Susan in her group home, including bringing holidays to her. Susan has a sister, Toni, who is five years older.

The cause of Susan's cerebral palsy (CP) was hypoxia. Doris was never told why the labor process was not normal, but Susan lost oxygen at birth, and she was not breathing when born during an emergency Cesarean. The doctors told Doris to "take her home and love her, and we'll see." She struggled with the "why" of the labor and delivery circumstances and Susan's subsequent abnormal development, and she described her coping strategy as "I clung to my faith and did what I had to do."

Susan began having seizures when she was three days old. The younger years were "extremely emotional" for Doris because of the nature of the intense care required. Doris held Susan in her lap and fed her every meal for many years. Susan was thought to be asthmatic until a diagnostic test revealed that when she swallowed food, it was going right into her lungs, which is aspiration. Now she is fed directly into the stomach via a feeding tube. The prognosis for Susan is uncertain. Her greatest vulnerability now is pneumonia because she easily goes into respiratory distress.

Doris's parents were not available for support when Susan was born. Her father had died before Susan was born, and her mother did not know how to cope, calling Susan's birth a "tragedy." When Susan was younger, Doris was self-conscious of having to take her around in a wheelchair. She had no awareness of CP and had few models of people in wheelchairs in public places. Friends did not understand why she could not take Susan skiing or camping with their families. She had hoped that mentally, Susan would "be okay, but some dreams did not come true." Doris had to come to terms with the reality that "my child is not like other children" and was finally able to accept this when Susan was six years old.

Raising Susan was difficult. Harry was in aviation maintenance; he was sometimes away on deployments for the Navy, and Toni was Doris's "right-hand girl." Doris went back to teaching when Susan started school at seven, and Toni helped take care of her sister on teacher work days, which were a few a year. The most difficult thing for Doris to overcome was that they were not a normal family. On the other hand, Doris felt blessed to be able to teach social studies, a subject she loved; she taught at a center for pregnant high school girls for thirteen years, and then she taught humanities at a local university for five years, after which she retired.

Until age sixteen, Susan lived in a three-bedroom home with her family. The house was modified and had a special bathroom, with an open shower and a bath chair. At age eighteen, Doris qualified for an intermediate care facility, and with the Medicaid waiver, she was able to move in 2009. When Doris moved to her current ICF, her parents downsized and moved to a condo—they now live less than a mile from Susan. Doris is grateful that her daughter has a good place to live. Susan goes to a day support program and on Sunday attends a nearby church. However, Doris is frustrated with some of the things not done in a timely manner at the home, like trimming Susan's nails. She was at a meeting in April when it was suggested for Susan to have an iPad, but that did not happen for six months.

The effect of having a sibling with a disability is often ignored. Toni has been married twice. She chose not to have children in her first marriage, directly related to being Susan's sister. I had no opportunity to interview Toni and so do not know the full story. After remarrying, Toni became a mom in 2012. Her son is a "miracle" baby, said Doris, as he had lymph fluid seeping into his lungs and was not expected to live. The leak was surgically plugged, and he is now fine. I can relate to Doris's joy, as I have healthy grandchildren; some had medical problems in the early weeks, but none were related to my son's disability.

Harry is calm and steady, Doris said. He provided a lot of mechanical adaptations so that Susan could live in their home when she was younger. She felt the hardest part still is getting beyond "Why?" and said there is no answer for that question.

## Common Concerns

Although Susan and Cathy are in wheelchairs and nonverbal, and my son Chris is ambulatory and verbal, I was struck by the similarities of concerns for care that I had in common with these moms. I can identify frustrating issues such as nails not being trimmed on time or a diet that promotes weight gain. We want our children to be cared for as we would care for them, if we were able to do so. I want my child to look as handsome and nicely dressed as possible. When parents see signs of lesser things not being tended to, like an overdue haircut, we wonder what else is not being taken care of by staff.

While I do not have the same mobility problems as Susan and Cathy in bringing Chris to my home for a visit or taking him places, we do not go to as many places as I would like to because of the lack of public family bathrooms. I'm not comfortable letting him use a men's room alone in a large venue, like a stadium. Also, I don't want him to wait alone while I use the ladies' room. Family bathrooms in airports and other places are a godsend and allow us to enjoy more outings together, but they are still not universal. However, I've noticed there are increasingly more family/assistance bathrooms in public spaces.

Amenities of life that most people take for granted, such as accessible, safe bathrooms, are not popular subjects for discussion. Most people are indifferent to these concerns, until they themselves need them. The following personal story illustrates how simple things are often made difficult, mainly because of a lack of understanding by others:

My church had a bathroom designated as a ladies' handicapped bathroom, close to other men's and women's bathrooms. We changed the sign on the door to make it a male/female bathroom, which made life easier for caregivers with opposite-gender children, disabled or not. However, it took six months of my constant vigilance (read nagging) to actually change the sign, once all relevant parties agreed. I take satisfaction in the many people who've benefitted from this simple change.

# Questions for Discussion or Self-Reflection

1.  Have you ever needed to make a change in an institution such as a house of worship or a school?

   _____

   _____

   _____

   _____

   _____

   _____

2.  How did you overcome resistance when you were trying to make a change to improve the lives of people with disabilities?

   _____

   _____

   _____

   _____

   _____

   _____

3.  What kind of needs did the Mother-Daughter Book Club fill?

   _____

   _____

_____

_____

_____

_____

_____

4.  How do you think the mothers benefitted? How did the daughters benefit?

_____

_____

_____

_____

_____

5.  There are often mixed feelings when an adult child with a disability lives out of the family home. What emotions do you think parents experience with such a situation?

_____

_____

_____

_____

_____

_____

# CHAPTER 4

## From Russia with Love

At our wedding, Roger and I introduced his three and my four children to our guests; he said, "Having children is like tearing out your heart and watching it walk around." The statement is even more true when your child has special needs. Giving birth puts most of us into super-protective mode; I realized early on that my most important job was to keep them all alive so they could take their own chances at age eighteen. Chris will never reach the eighteen-year-old freedom level like his brothers, and his dependency is my heart walking around and feeling very vulnerable.

*Irene, Bob, Zoe, and Zachary are fictional names.*

Irene and Bob have been friends of mine for about eight years. I was aware that their two children were adopted from Russia and had differing levels of special needs, but I didn't know the fascinating story of their adoption. The story of their parenting their adult children is even more heartrending; they traveled so far and went through so much to complete their family.

Irene and Bob had been married for fifteen years and were childless. In 1992, they began to explore adoption. Irene's brother had adopted two foster boys in the United States, and issues of parental rights arose from the birth parents. Irene and Bob wanted to avoid any problems of that sort, and they also wanted to adopt a white child because they did not feel equipped to handle the issues of parenting a child of color (twenty-five years ago, mixed-race families were far less common than they are today). In order to adopt from Russia, they utilized Catholic Family Services, although they are not Catholic. That affiliation was necessary because in order to use a Russian specialization service, they had to go through a US agency. They applied for adoption on the day after Thanksgiving 1992.

In the spring of 1993, Irene and Bob traveled to Moscow; they were instructed to wear only old clothes, so as not to give an impression of being wealthy Americans and thus vulnerable to criminals. They had cash strapped to their bodies, and they had brought an empty baby carrier. It was unpopular for Americans to adopt Russians, and they had to pass by armed KGB guards to enter the adoption office to sign their required papers. They stayed in the apartment of a widow and her two daughters for their first few days. This host family was part of the program. Irene recalled nice peasant food and warmth from their hosts. She considered it a good omen that this was the first year that the government allowed Orthodox Russians to celebrate Easter, and there were banners everywhere, proclaiming in Russian, "Christ is Lord."

After the first few days, they flew to Saransk on a bare-bones airline (Irene's description), complete with live chickens. They were in Saransk for two weeks, and their hotel was a half-hour ride to the orphanage. Irene recalled a great deal of complicated paperwork at the American Embassy. They also had to follow strict protocols in Russia. They were told to bring many gifts of consumer goods of specific types and prices to give out to several people. The higher the level of official to be compensated (bribed), the higher the price of the gift.

It did not help that a local political coup occurred while they were in Russia; the new local government did not want to process the papers. To get the papers signed, the coordinator went to the government office every day for a week; she was finally able to get the required signatures. Irene and Bob were both ill during this time, adding to their stress.

They were able to adopt a daughter, who was born in July 1993. She was two months premature, weighed two-and-a-half pounds at birth, and her given name was Ruby. She had been in a Russian hospital from July to the end of November and then was brought to the orphanage in Saransk. Information about the mother came by word of mouth; her mother was an orphan with little education and possibly mentally challenged. The doctor Irene and Bob were working with said that the mother was raped, perhaps by someone in the Russian military.

According to the foundation's rules, all children who were adopted had disabilities. Irene and Bob knew they were taking a risk but also knew that children put up for adoption were screened; those who were most likely to have a chance were allowed to be adopted. The orphanage was very poor, and the children had no toys, but it was clear to Irene that the girl had been held often and was loved by the staff. The orphanage had no diapers, and Irene recalls that the first time she held the baby, who had no hair and big blue eyes, she peed on her. She jokingly said that this may have been a forecasting of what life was going to be like.

They were also supposed to bring home a four-year-old boy with them, but his grandmother had come to visit him, violating the rule that children were not supposed to have any living family members in order to be adopted. That made him ineligible for adoption. However, there was a second boy available, and Irene and Bob were told they could come for him later. Irene recalled being terrified when the time came to take Zoe (their name for Ruby) home to America; her experience with children was limited, and she had to learn quickly. They arrived home, pleasantly surprised to find their house full of parenting and baby books, gifts, and food from neighbors, church members, and friends.

In October of that same year, Zachary was available for adoption, and Bob traveled to Russia to bring him home (Irene had to stay home with Zoe). Zachary had a stroke at birth. He was then sent immediately to an orphanage in Murmansk, which was more economically advantaged than Zoe's orphanage. Zachary had toys and therapy. This was "Zachary #3," as two other boys who were promised did not materialize. Bob came home with two-and-a-half-year-old Zachary, while Irene was dealing with Zoe's first ear infection.

In October 1993, they went to church with both children; it was World Communion Sunday in the Methodist church and the first Sunday they brought both children to the service. Irene and Bob were surprised to see about fifty people visiting from Russia on an exchange program with the Orthodox Church. Irene and Bob brought the two children forward for a blessing; later, they hosted an impromptu Sunday afternoon reception in their home. They had a baby, a new toddler who did not speak any English, and a houseful of American and Russian guests.

Both Zachary and Zoe were enrolled in various schools and programs, both private and public, to deal with their special needs. They've had occupational therapy, physical therapy, and speech therapy; they were diagnosed with attention deficit hyperactivity disorder (ADHD). In preschool, Zachary was also diagnosed as dyslexic. Zoe was enrolled in an infant stimulation program until age two, and then she attended a public elementary school. Both children eventually attended a private school specializing in children with ADHD. Both Zachary and Zoe also had daycare with a private provider in their home, as Irene and Bob both worked full-time. Each child attended and graduated from a private high school.

In 2002, Bob had a stroke, which significantly changed the family. At the time, Irene was away on a business trip, and both children were home with Bob. The children did not realize what had happened. Bob had been in good health, and the stroke, which was completely unexpected, occurred during the night. Irene did not get home until the next afternoon; she was unable to get Bob to the hospital within the window for treatment that would mitigate the effects of the stroke. Bob had to close his practice as an optometrist and became disabled himself. Zachary noted that "Dad had a stroke, just like me." Since that time, Zoe has been very protective of Bob.

Zachary graduated from college and is working. The main focus of the family at present is helping Zoe to become more responsible, independent, and employed. Irene stated that Zoe has come further than she ever thought she would, but she's still concerned that if she's not with family, she could easily be taken advantage of. Zoe attends a different church than her parents and meets with a group of people her age there. She has a good friend who wrote a college application essay entitled, "What I Learned from Zoe," but this friend is now away at school.

Zoe does have marketable skills; she volunteered for three years at an elementary school cafeteria and was a volunteer at a summer program in a private school. She is currently job hunting. Irene is trying to balance helping Zoe look for a job with encouraging her to look for a position on her own. She also tries to help Zoe with dressing appropriately for an interview and coaching her on interview skills but doesn't want her to think that she is being critical of her. She gently nudges her to write thank you notes after interviews and follow up if she doesn't hear back from the employer. Irene's wishes are that Zoe has a fulfilling life. She does drive, which is an asset in having a steady job.

Irene and Bob are people of faith and are active in their church community. They are both caring and giving people. I asked Irene how her faith helped support her with Zoe, and to my surprise, she responded with something I once told her regarding what I felt the Lord said about my own son: "I love him more than you ever could, and I will provide for him." She stated that this keeps her believing that things will work out well for both of her children. She also has found some new ways to relate to Zoe, which has been an ongoing problem. Zoe has always identified with Bob more than with Irene, sometimes even being quite disparaging to her.

Irene told me about altercasting, a technique she uses with Zoe. Irene asks Zoe, "Are you willing ..." to do whatever is required, telling her exactly what is needed to be done and why, and including a positive statement of how she sees her skills and assets.(1)

Zoe does not qualify for assistance for disability because she was not formally diagnosed with an intellectual or developmental disability before age eighteen. She is currently one of those people who fall through the holes in the health care net. She has some independence but does not yet have a full set of skills of an independent adult. Irene feels that she has tried everything to help Zoe, but she is still not where she needs to be. For the future, Zachary will be her guardian when her parents are no longer around; Irene's brother will also be Zoe's guardian.

## Overseas Adoptions

Intercountry adoption is under the purview of the Bureau of Consular Affairs, US Department of State. Laws of the federal government, the state where the parents reside, and the country where the adopted child resides must all be satisfied. Also, if the child's home country is a part of the Hague Adoption Convention, which covers ninety countries, their policies must also be followed.

To adopt a child from overseas, adoptive parents must be US citizens. If unmarried, the parent must be at least twenty-five years old. If married, the parents must jointly adopt the child, even if they are separated but not yet divorced. There are other requirements such as background checks, fingerprinting, and a home study. The process can take up to four years or longer.(2)

Terri Bell has worked with over a thousand families for over thirty years in the field of adopting international special needs children. In a 2006 posting on her website, she wrote that there are no absolutes in these types of adoptions. She listed the many variables:

- the adoption program itself
- the medical expertise available
- the medical facilities used
- cultural understandings
- the capabilities of each overseas agency
- the expertise of the US agency that represents the family overseas.

She also noted that some families request to adopt children with special needs, while others may want a particular child and then find out it has special needs.(3)

Bob and Irene are courageous people who made a commitment to their adopted children, no matter what the circumstances. They have my admiration and respect for what they went through to create their family and for their ongoing commitment to the well-being of their adult children. They did not choose an easy path to becoming parents but are steadfast in their ongoing parenting.

# Questions for Discussion or Self-Reflection

1. Is the task of parenting in this situation more difficult because these children were adopted?

   _____

   _____

   _____

   _____

   _____

   _____

2. How can an overseas adoption add to challenges in parenting?

   _____

   _____

   _____

   _____

   _____

   _____

3. What are the strengths of the parents in this chapter?

   _____

   _____

   _____

_____

_____

_____

_____

_____

4. What skills does a child need to achieve total independence?

_____

_____

_____

_____

_____

5. How much more does a parent have to do to ensure success for an adult child without a diagnosis, which can provide federal and state assistance?

_____

_____

_____

_____

_____

## CHAPTER 5

### *Interviews at Sea*

*All names in this chapter are fictitious.*

In 2015 and 2016, I took cruises to Bermuda, and on each, I interviewed a mom of an adult with disabilities. Neither interview was prearranged, and I considered both chance meetings as serendipity. In 2015, I was standing in line at the ship's dining room, waiting to be seated for brunch, when I noticed Laurie and her parents, Peggy and Joe, behind me. After introducing myself, I told Peggy and Joe that I was writing a book about adults with disabilities and asked if I could interview them later. They agreed, and Peggy and I met the next day.

In 2016, I told some friends about the next cruise, and they signed up, along with members of their extended family. Because my roommate had to cancel at the last minute, those friends graciously invited me to share several meals and activities with them. Adam, a young man with Down syndrome, and his mother, Janell, were in that family group.

There were similarities in both of these families. The adults with disabilities were in their thirties and had traveled with their parents to many places. They both had many skills and showed a lot of independence, and their parents were counting on siblings to oversee their care after the parents are deceased. However, similarities ended there. Laurie lived with her parents, and her friends and social group were her parents, while Adam had friends of his own and lived in a condo three blocks from his mom. Yet, in some respects, the stories of these families have much in common.

## Peggy, Joe, and Laurie

Laurie's parents have been married for over forty years. Their two sons, aged forty-one and thirty-eight, are married and live out of state. Laurie and her parents are a constant threesome. They enjoy many trips together, and the center of their social life is a boat club. All of the boat club members are similar in age to Peggy and Joe and are also Laurie's social circle. Peggy and Joe do not belong to any other organizations, nor do they belong to a church, but they do believe in God.

Laurie was born prematurely in December 1981, weighing only three pounds, fourteen ounces, possibly due to Peggy having eclampsia while pregnant. At six weeks of age, Laurie had pneumonia and had to be hospitalized for a while. Peggy claims that upon release from the hospital, Laurie was a "different baby." She did not walk until age two. She attended a school at age three and was diagnosed with cerebral palsy. She is also profoundly deaf and wears two hearing aids. She had scoliosis and had to wear a brace for a time. She has a short stature and a fused spine, and Peggy speculated that perhaps Laurie's problems are genetic, as she herself has a sister with dwarfism.

When Laurie was ten, she was officially diagnosed as mildly intellectually disabled. When she was mainstreamed in school, she felt isolated and did not make friends. Unfortunately, she experienced some bullying in school; someone once put gum in her hair.

Laurie has many skills and interests. She plays computer games, uses email, and watches YouTube videos and the news. She cooks, does laundry, and makes greeting cards using a craft cutter machine. She also enjoys doing her own hair, choosing her clothing, cooking, and making a variety of crafts. She takes care of one of the family's dogs and a cat, and she is in a book club. Peggy and Joe previously took Laurie on a Disney cruise ship, and she easily found her own way around the ship.

Peggy reassures Laurie that she can stay home alone, if necessary. She is confident that Laurie knows how to handle emergencies, because she demonstrated her skill at age ten when she called 911 because her brothers, while playing with her, put her in a closet. She was not standing for that kind of behavior from the boys, playful or not.

Both parents have some physical issues and are aware of their own aging, accompanied by concern about care for Laurie when they have passed. Peggy is a survivor of fallopian cancer and has limited range of motion in her right arm due to a rod inserted after a fracture, and Joe had a quadruple heart bypass.

When I asked her what carried her through the days, Peggy said that she considered Laurie "a blessing, an angel." She said that when Laurie dies, it will "leave a big hole in the universe." She says she stopped crying five years ago over what might have been regarding Laurie; she's focused on the present and future. If Joe dies first and she doesn't feel able to stay in their home, she hopes to be able to move into assisted living with her daughter.

Plans for Laurie's future are in place. She will live with one of her brothers after her parents die or are unable to care for her any longer. When Peggy had cancer surgery, she was concerned about Laurie, even though Joe was there to help. She's not sure that Laurie living with the brother will really work out. His family has young children, and she cannot picture what the household would look like with the addition of Laurie. She also worried that Laurie will not have friends if she's no longer connected to the boat club.

Laurie is one of those individuals on the cusp of being independent but not quite fully so. Because she's lived at home for her whole life, they haven't explored programs that might place her into a suitable job or a residence. It's not easy to integrate another adult into a sibling's home when that adult has no other connections in the community except the sibling's family. It can put a burden on that family to become a person's entire social support system. A family bringing an adult sibling who has a disability into their family should consider how they can balance their own children's school, sports, and social needs while providing a life for the sibling. They would have to think through how the person with a disability could feel isolated and lonely, being removed from their former social life. It would be a major adjustment from being the sole focus of the parents' attention for so many years, but now having to share attention with nephews and nieces.

However, the situation could be positive as well as negative. In this new setting, a person's world could shrink, or there could be new opportunities for social contacts. In addition, a person with a disability newly placed in a sibling's home may not feel as comfortable staying home alone all day if both spouses are working; a day program may offer more socialization.

In all fairness, I didn't have an opportunity to interview the son, as he was not on the ship, and Peggy didn't offer his contact information. Perhaps he's explored opportunities in the community for Laurie for when that time comes, which would be ideal. At any rate, the transition of living without her parents and having to leave her home and friends suddenly would not be easy, for her or for anyone in that situation.

As we talked, I felt that Peggy was starting to think about the implications of her plans and consider that perhaps she and Joe hadn't made the best choice for Laurie's future. I was privileged to have met this family and learn of their lives, but I fear I may have caused some distress by raising the topic of the future while they were on their vacation. Perhaps that was my own perception of the situation. When two people converse, there is always something new created, if only in the moment. Obviously, I didn't intend harm of any kind. The best I can hope for is that through the interview, the parents gained some new ideas that will add positively to their planning for their daughter.

## Janell and Adam

Adam's story demonstrates careful planning and independence for adulthood for a person with a disability. Adam was born in April 1980. At two months of age, he was diagnosed with Down syndrome trisomy 21.(1) By her own admission, Janell, his mother, was "totally devastated" by this news. One pediatrician advised her to put Adam into a home for children with disabilities. Another doctor, however, told her to take him home and see what she could do with him. She was not sure that she would be able to meet his needs, especially because she had a fifteen-year-old daughter who was experiencing what she called "typical teen problems." However, his sister "adored" him from the start, and raising Adam has always been, as Janell describes it, "easy." That sister is now married, and she and her husband have no children. Adam's father died in 2010.

Adam lives in his own condo, a few blocks from where he works at the YMCA and a few blocks from his mother's condo. He started working as a volunteer at the Y in 1999 after graduating from high school with a regular diploma. At graduation, he received one of only twenty faculty awards given out. He was enrolled in a state university program that had classes for people with disabilities, but that program no longer exists. He attended a community college, taking general classes. After only eight months at the YMCA, his status was changed from volunteer to paid employee. His work included filing in the corporate office, and now he is in guest relations and housekeeping. He is proud of his job and enjoys his work. Adam's routine includes Sunday morning workouts at the Y. He has had a girlfriend for the past nineteen years who also has Down syndrome, and he also gets together with his best friend of many years. He also participates in numerous family get-togethers.

In addition to being Adam's advocate, education advisor, and supporter, Janell was an activist for children with Down syndrome. In 1981, she began a Down syndrome support group for parents, and many of those parents still meet, but she stopped being involved in an official capacity five years ago.

Her advocacy began when it was time for Adam to attend public school. She wasn't comfortable with him going to school full-time after being in an infant stimulation program, so she arranged for him to attend school two days a week when he was two years old and three days a week at age three; at age four, he started going every day. Until high school, he attended special classes for speech. Throughout his elementary school years, Janell cooperated with the school to choose a teacher compatible with Adam's learning style. In high school, she helped him choose academic classes to suit his interests. He never asked for accommodations for special needs.

Adam stated, "I loved high school. Senior English was my favorite, and math was my strongest subject."

I enjoyed meals and some leisure time with Adam during the cruise. He has an engaging personality and is clever. I was on his team in a shipboard version of Trivial Pursuit, and he helped our team with several answers. On another occasion, I enjoyed watching him order a specialty drink to share with his aunt; he was adamant about paying for it.

At one point in the interview, Janell had Adam leave the room so we could talk in private. I asked her about future plans for Adam; she said she had not yet set up a special needs trust (SNT), just a regular trust with her daughter as trustee. She indicated that the Achieving a Better Life Experience (ABLE) Act was a godsend for putting money into savings. (2) Adam, who is good with money, pays his own bills and has his own health insurance through his job. He also gets over twenty days a year of paid vacation, which she sees as a real benefit. They often travel together, including taking a river cruise in Europe. Adam later told me that he likes river cruises better than the larger cruise ships.

Janell had some opinions on benefits available today for families, some of which may be seen as controversial. She disliked the concept of Medicaid waivers for young children with Down syndrome that allowed in-home aides, because she felt that the money could be better used elsewhere. We discussed the reality that many mothers are now working or have other children and need these aides. She herself did not return to work until Adam was ten years old. She worked in her father's company, which allowed her to have more job flexibility. When I was in graduate school, I had to pay for respite care and afterschool programs for Chris; we did not benefit from Medicaid waivers of that type, as they didn't exist at the time. I told her I thought I would have taken advantage of them had they been available. She also felt that having aides in regular classrooms for children with disabilities who are in inclusion programs brings about resentment by others, because these children seem to get special treatment and take away from teachers' time with the other children. That may be the case for some, but I've also heard of great experiences in inclusion programs from both teachers and parents. As my own son is long past school age, I could not offer any opinion based on experience because he was never in inclusion programs.

We finished our interview on a positive note. Janelle mentioned a favorite poster she had seen of two children fishing side by side; one of them has Down syndrome, and the title was "Friends Don't Count Chromosomes." I fully agree.

## About Down Syndrome

According to the Mayo Clinic website, Down syndrome is one of the best known causes of disability, perhaps because it is the most identifiable and the most prevalent. Down syndrome comes from a variation of chromosome 21, caused by abnormal cell division. People with Down syndrome usually have mild to moderate cognitive impairment. There are three genetic variations of Down syndrome: Trisomy 21, which accounts for 95 percent of all cases of Down syndrome, Mosaic Down syndrome, and Translocation 21 Down syndrome. People with Down syndrome can be expected to live to over sixty, depending on their particular health problems, which can be heart defects, spinal problems, sleep apnea, obesity, dementia, Alzheimer's, immune disorders, gastrointestinal defects, endocrine system problems, and dental/hearing/vision issues.(3)

# Questions for Discussion or Self-Reflection

1. What has contributed to Adam having such a good life?

_____

_____

_____

_____

_____

_____

_____

_____

_____

_____

2. What will Laurie's parents have to put in place to ensure she has a secure and enjoyable life?

_____

_____

_____

_____

_____

_____

_____

_____

3. What do you need to do to prepare for your child's future?

_____

_____

_____

_____

_____

_____

_____

_____

4. What are the pros and cons of Adam's current situation? Of Laurie's?

_____

_____

_____

_____

_____

_____

## CHAPTER 6

# *Caring Families Come in All Shapes and Sizes*

*All names in this chapter are fictitious.*

The two families I interviewed for this chapter lived in very different circumstances but had in common a strong desire to do what was best for their child, often making sacrifices of time, money, or lifestyle. Both fathers in these families are retired Navy veterans.

## Rennae and Donna

I interviewed Rennae in her cozy living room with her twenty-one-year-old daughter, Donna, and two large dogs, a fifty-pound part-border collie and a seventy-pound boxer mix. The dogs greeted me at the door enthusiastically and continued to be curious about me for the first half of the interview, climbing on my lap and punctuating the conversation with barking at outside passersby, until Rennae led them to the back yard. Donna, who becomes upset when she hears shrill voices of little children, was not fazed at all by the dogs' barking. Her selective reaction to varying noises illustrates the idiosyncratic nature of autism and the difficulty of finding appropriate treatment and education for people on the spectrum. People with autism have a variety of symptoms and need their own individualized treatment plans.

Donna was a bit fussy, perhaps anxious, during the interview and asked Mom to "scratch." In response, Rennae scratched her back a bit and then rubbed Donna's feet for the rest of the interview. Donna was calm for the remaining time.

Rennae is a single mother, and Donna is an only child. In 2006, Rennae and her spouse, Jake, separated, but they are not divorced. Jake is still very much involved with Donna. He is retired military, lives nearby, and works as a letter carrier. Rennae's house is on his route, and he stops in to see Donna almost daily. He also is a caregiver for her when needed and accompanies Rennae to Donna's medical appointments (she needs his help to manage her). Donna only speaks occasionally and is not toilet trained.

Jake's girlfriend can be considered a part of this family. In fact, the larger of the dogs belonged to Jake's girlfriend, as Rennae was dog-sitting. Jake's girlfriend also is involved with Donna and asks Rennae for tips on how to care for her when Donna visits with her and Jake. This may seem like a complex family relationship, but it works in providing for Donna's needs. There are no siblings and no other family nearby who could be of help to Rennae. This arrangement is a creative solution for Donna's care.

In December 1994, Donna was born at thirty-eight weeks, with no apparent problems. At one year, she began saying words but then stopped speaking at eighteen months. She walked a bit late but not significantly so, according to Rennae. When Donna was two years old, a neighbor who was a teacher told Rennae about testing and early intervention and suggested she pursue this route for her daughter. Rennae went to her doctor to get a prescription for the early intervention program, as this was required at the time. Jake was at sea, and she was alone to hear the doctor's diagnosis: mental disability. In the early intervention program, someone mentioned autism to her, and she started reading about the disorder. The more she read, the more she understood that this diagnosis could apply to Donna. Six months later, she returned to the doctor with this new knowledge, and as she had surmised, the diagnosis was autism.

Sadly, I still hear from parents of young children about the length of time it takes to get a proper diagnosis for their child. Part of the problem may be that as children grow, developmental lags become more apparent;

it takes a while for the entire picture to emerge. Another factor may be the reluctance of doctors to diagnose young children and provide a label that may not be correct. I could see developmental delays in Chris and brought them to the attention of doctors but was told that I was just a "worried mother." When he was three years old, I found a doctor able to tell me the truth, and once I had a name (even though it was a vague "mental disability"), I felt able to move forward in his best interests.

Donna progressed through programs in the public school system, where she was largely in self-contained special education classrooms, except for occasionally being included in regular music and physical education classes. She attended summer sessions at school and some private camps, until her behaviors and her sensitivity to certain noises canceled those options.

Donna is currently in transition. Although she was eligible to attend public school for one more school year, Rennae decided not to send her. Donna was resisting school attendance, and according to Rennae, it was "hard to get her to go."

Rennae is now looking into the combination of a home care provider for mornings and day support program for afternoons. This kind of support would provide continuity of care, social interaction, and a schedule for Rennae to rely upon for her own part-time work as a church secretary. She would also have time to attend to her own routines and necessities of life. Donna does not sleep through the night, and subsequently, neither can Rennae.

Recently, Donna spent three months at a residential rehabilitation hospital about a hundred miles from home; she had been hitting and kicking others and had great anxiety, which exacerbated her acting-out behaviors. Rennae said that placing Donna out of the home, even though temporary, was the hardest thing she ever did. However, the results were worth it. Donna's medication was adjusted, and she received treatment that helped with the behaviors. Rennae and Jake visited Donna every weekend, bringing her a new stuffed animal each time. Donna was happy to see them but was not clingy. She let them know when it was time to leave; Rennae was gratified to learn that her daughter could adjust to being without her if necessary, which was a nice surprise.

Although there was not a drastic improvement, Donna was doing better, primarily because of the medication change. However, some problematic behaviors still persist. Donna is anxious that she might hear a noise if she goes outside. Rennae cannot take her to the beach anymore, which both of them enjoyed, nor can she take her to church on Sunday. When she recently tried to attend the Wednesday night service at church, Donna refused to get out of the car. In the past, Donna had enjoyed this service, particularly joining in the singing.

Donna did do well, however, on a trip to a pumpkin patch, sitting in the patch and handling pumpkins one by one. At home and at day programs, she still hits or pinches people, and she throws things. Several of their televisions have met a sad end after Donna pushed them off the stands. The TV now sits on the floor, with a large pillow in front of it.

Rennae takes Donna to a church-related group in the area; when Donna meets someone, she asks people their names and then says, "What color?" meaning what color are their eyes. She has a few friends her age who also have autism, but they do not interact except to sit and watch TV together.

Rennae feels that throughout Donna's life, she just finishes fighting one battle and has to go on to the next, and "battle to battle" is now the norm. Her present focus is on finding the right combination of proper care for Donna. Care for adults depends on having Medicaid waivers available and finding the right program. She has a waiver that pays for companion care from 10 a.m. to 2 p.m. Donna expresses in her own way that she does not want both Mom and caregiver in the home at the same time, only one or the other, and Rennae tries to structure her day accordingly.

Rennae says she would love to occasionally get away for a weekend. Once a year, she takes a trip to California to see her family, and Jake takes care of Donna. However, even then, she is caregiving because Jake calls her with emergency situations, which he has to handle until she returns. We discussed Donna's future, including the ultimate question: what happens when she and Jake are no longer able to care for their daughter? Rennae does have a will and a trust, but she was not sure what kind of trust. I informed her about Survivor Benefits Plan (SBP) trusts, which she qualified for since Jake is retired military and Donna is his beneficiary. Rennae was not aware of the Military Child Protection Act, legislation passed in 2014 that provides the ability to set up an SBP trust. She assumed the SBP would go directly to Donna but was not aware that her Medicaid would be wiped out by these payments if she didn't put them into a trust. We also discussed the difference between a will and a revocable trust for parental assets, and Rennae indicated that she's been planning to look at legal issues.

Rennae is not alone in taking time to organize all the legal details in the event of one's death or incapacitation. It took me about two years to decide how to do things and select the right attorney. Rennae ideally would like Donna to remain in her home, and we discussed the ramifications of that situation, including twenty-four-hour care for Donna, house repairs, and upkeep. Rennae also mentioned obtaining a residential waiver and finding another place for Donna, a major step because Rennae's cottage-style house has always been her home. As parents, we have to think through so many scenarios to make the right decision; it can be overwhelming. We can become so stressed that we postpone making necessary decisions rather than make the wrong choice.

Rennae spoke affirmatively about encouragement from her faith community, a congregation of about seventy-five members. Her pastors have always been supportive, and the women in her Bible study understand her situation; she can talk with them about her life. They also pray with her, which is important to her. She mentioned throughout the interview that she prays often to get through all the circumstances of life, especially the unexpected and unplanned. Two Bible passages that are of comfort to Rennae are Philippians 3:14: "I press toward the mark for the prize of the high calling of God in Christ Jesus," and Psalm 46:10: "Be still and know that I am God."

## Paul, Harry, and Kyle

Paul also experienced several crisis moments in the lives of his two sons. I interviewed him in his home, which has a view of the Atlantic Ocean from his comfortable, expansive living room. He inherited the house from his mother and completely remodeled it. In September 1971, the day before Paul deployed to Vietnam as a naval aviator on board the USS *Constellation*, Harry was born. It became apparent that he had some kind of developmental disability when he was between eighteen and twenty-four months old. Paul's mother's brother was in care in a state home at the time, and they thought that perhaps this was a genetic disorder, but the chromosome test did not show abnormalities. No further genetic diagnosis was ever made.

Paul's son Kyle was born in November 1974 and had the same problems as Harry. Paul and his wife divorced in 1978, and she remarried in 1979, when she was living with their sons in the southern part of the United States. Paul remained in the Navy but always attempted to see his sons as much as possible. He flew to see his sons when his schedule allowed, but when he arrived, his ex-wife often refused to let him see them. When Hurricane Katrina hit in 2005, the boys were living in a group home in the area and were evacuated to another city. The family later moved to the Midwest. Paul's sons are now living in group homes, one block apart from each other and twenty-five minutes away from their mother. They see their mom every other weekend, and Paul visits them often.

I asked Paul how he dealt with being away from his sons who have disabilities. He said that as a Navy pilot, he had learned to compartmentalize and therefore did no grieving. He felt that as an absent father, his biggest challenge was balancing everyone's needs. In the 1990s, he became concerned about what would happen to his sons if something happened to him. He related a "titanic" legal battle with his ex-wife's parents, who were caring for Harry at the time; he tried to convince them that accepting Supplemental Security Income (SSI) when Harry turned eighteen was in his best interest; doing so would enable him to receive Medicaid. They didn't understand the benefits of Medicaid versus Paul's direct monetary support, which was cash but with no accompanying services. The grandparents finally acquiesced, and Harry received SSI. Paul also set up a trust to continue to make cash contributions to both Harry and Kyle.

While setting up the trust for the boys, Paul had to find a lot of information on his own. His own attorney was not familiar with the process. He learned how to provide for his sons' future, and after retiring from the Navy, he decided to become a financial planner. As word of his expertise grew, 40 percent of his clients were involved with special needs trusts. Consequently, he was invited to speak at many venues on the topic, including at the Judge Advocate General's Core School to instruct Navy personnel on the topic. Paul noted that in reviewing over a hundred special needs trusts over the years, he found many errors. He is currently a trustee for a special needs community trust, which is one asset I set up for my son many years ago.

Because of his profession, Paul was well aware of the Survivors Benefit Law of 2016; it was through his newsletter that I learned about it. Retired military members can now choose to put SBP payments into a special needs trust (SNT) for their special needs child. These funds do not count when calculating the limits for receiving SSI and Medicaid.(1), (2)

Paul and I discussed the two most traumatic events for people with special needs: when the parents die, and when they have to move away from the family home. He stated that it is much more traumatic when those situations occur simultaneously; that is, when the last parent dies and the person with a disability has to be relocated in an emergency situation. When Paul speaks to groups, he tells stories of the successful transitions of adults who move to group homes when there is no crisis; he gives examples of how those people have developed and grown through the process, much more than anyone ever expected. He showed me a video of Kyle doing his Michael Jackson routine, encouraged by his group home, to illustrate the home's benefits.

In contrast to his experience with his own sons, Paul is now helping to raise his current wife's two grandchildren, ages eight and twelve, who live with them. He feels he is making up for lost time fathering with his participation in all of the activities that he missed with his own children, such as school and sports; he enjoys this new role.

# Questions for Group Discussion or Self-Reflection

1. Each of these two families has birth parents with very different arrangements. What common denominators do you see in both?

_____

_____

_____

_____

_____

_____

_____

_____

_____

2. What might be major concerns for Rennae for Donna's future?

_____

_____

_____

_____

_____

_____

_____

3. What factors do divorced or separated parents need to keep in mind for co-parenting their child with a disability?

_____

_____

_____

_____

_____

_____

_____

_____

_____

4. If you are divorced or separated, what works best for you in co-parenting? What are the biggest challenges?

_____

_____

_____

_____

_____

_____

_____

_____

# CHAPTER 7

## *A Home of One's Own*

Linda and Terry Ritter have been my friends for over thirty years. Chris and their daughter Kim both attended a self-contained school for special education. Linda and I also served for several years on a special education advisory board for our city's schools.

Kim is a few years older than Chris. Her disabilities are more severe, and she is in a wheelchair. When she was fifty, a correct diagnosis was finally found: Dandy-Walker malformation, which involves the small size and abnormal position of the middle of the cerebellum and other features. Her eyes are a bit wide, and she has an overbite, both part of the syndrome.(1)

Kim was born via a C-section, a "beautiful, perfect baby," according to Linda. She stayed in the hospital for ten days, and during that time, Kim was a demonstration baby for other mothers learning how to bathe their infants. However, Kim had sucking problems while nursing, and her head would droop while she was being burped. Terry and Linda later realized that she was having seizures. Linda said that because they were first-time parents, they missed developmental cues, such as thinking that they were doing the right thing by letting her scream in her crib until she fell asleep.

Kim started school before Public Law 94-142 (the Education for All Children with Disabilities Act, now the IDEA Act), mandating education for all students with disabilities, was passed in 1975.(2) Linda is a former teacher who fought to get her daughter's educational needs met, as have so many special needs parents. She was able to get her daughter speech therapy at age five, for example, when those were not normal services in the public schools.

Terry and Linda have been married for fifty-six years and have always shared the same standards and values, which is a source of the strength of their relationship. They chose to have two more children after Kim so there would be caregivers to share the responsibility of caring for their sister after the parents were no longer able to do so. They tried to provide a normal way of life whenever they could for their family; they didn't want any of their children to miss out on anything because of Kim. They didn't want her two sisters to feel left out, even though it was sometimes impossible for even one parent to be at a school or sports event.

The Ritters chose to establish a microboard in order to give Kim her own home and own life. Two components made it possible for Kim to have her own home. The first was the microboard, a legal entity that continues throughout Kim's life, with Kim's two sisters and some family friends. The board meets once a year (sometimes electronically) to discuss life planning issues, programs, and Kim's current needs. The second component, made possible by a state grant, was the purchase of a house, with the microboard as the owner. The microboard hires the caregiver, and Kim's Medicaid waiver pays for services. If so desired, other persons with disabilities could also reside at the house and pay rent. Terry and Linda are pioneers in establishing a microboard that encompasses home ownership.(3)

Linda and Terry have a sense of peace, knowing that Kim will always have a home, no matter what happens to them. In fact, the impetus to move Kim out of the family home, where she had always lived, was that Terry had a heart attack. The Ritters faced the reality, as we all must, that as we age, caring for a special needs adult child becomes physically more demanding, and we can no longer do the job alone.

Having the home for Kim, however, was not always easy. At the time of our interview, there was a problem with the caregiver, and they needed to hire a new person. Over the Christmas holiday, they had to have Kim in their own home for three weeks and take over caregiving duties themselves until they found a suitable new person. Care for Kim was not a simple task, as they had to widen doorframes in the home to accommodate her wheelchair. Both of them were exhausted after this period of caregiving.

In her own house, the microboard had freedom to provide what Kim needed and wanted. For example, for her fiftieth birthday party, Big Bird made an appearance. Linda pointed out that people who consider themselves politically correct might say this was not age appropriate. However, it pleased Kim, as the Muppet was one of her favorite characters and was appropriate for her, even if not necessarily for her chronological age. Political correctness aside, who wouldn't like to have Big Bird show up at their birthday?

Linda's biggest fear was lack of continuity of care when she and Terry are no longer there. The daughters, who both live out of state, will become Kim's legal guardians, while the others on the microboard are a backup. She was concerned about bills being paid on time, the proper management of the home, and annual licensure paperwork being properly completed. Kim has the Medicaid waiver for her lifetime, but Linda was concerned that the proper ongoing training for future caregivers may not be completed as required.

Linda said she was "over it" in fighting battles for Kim, as so many of us are, but yet we keep rallying to do what is necessary for our children, as long as we are able. Knowing Kim's care is secure allows Linda and Terry to enjoy their retirement, travelling and attending local cultural events. When asked about the couple's faith perspective, Linda said they could not credit faith in their parenting of Kim but felt that "having strong paternal and maternal instincts and a hope in things working out" was a key. Despite that seemingly secular stance, she added that they often prayed for strength and guidance to do the right thing. They continue to ask why Kim was disabled but have never received an answer. Their "how" is day-to-day surviving. In retrospect, Linda said that while some families may seem perfect to outsiders, everyone has some kind of problem.

## Postscript

Kim died eighteen months after this interview, on June 27, 2017 (her fifty-fourth birthday), following a three-week illness. On that last day, the nurses brought in a birthday cake, and Kim's last meal was frosting from her cake.

I attended her moving and inspirational funeral on August 12, 2017. The title on the church program was "A Liturgy of Thanksgiving to God for the Life of Kimberly Ann Ritter." Linda was being modest when she minimized the role of faith in caring for their daughter. In the eulogy, the pastor spoke about the love and concern that Kim always showed to others, even with her limited vocabulary. Only someone who was lovingly cared for could share love with others. Some people are reluctant to speak of their faith journey, but I know that Linda always advocated for Kimmy and did her best for her with a sense of hope. The pastor spoke of Kimmy's Confirmation in the church, and at the funeral, it was clear from the love and support of those who attended that this family was an engaged part of the congregation.

Her two sisters spoke of the many good times and specific remembrances they had of Kim, some humorous and some poignant. When Kim's cremains were laid to rest in the columbarium on church grounds, her favorite baby doll was included in the niche. For me, it was an emotional, overwhelming moment; I wondered what I would do and how our family would feel if we were in this situation.

Kim's death was a relief from caregiving, but as the pastor said in his homily, "For these parents, it is a peace that their child is safely at rest, in God's hands and care." Parents who are aging and are concerned about their child's future sometimes say they hope their child dies before they do, to relieve them of the anxiety and worry. In a 2013 report by Christine Towers, a parent was quoted as saying, "I think no other group of people in the world wishes their child to die before they do—but for parents of someone with high support needs, it is very worrying that they will be left with no one to make sure they are happy, loved, and cherished as full human beings."(4) This viewpoint is not often addressed in stories about people with disabilities, nor have I ever seen it on a program at a conference. Parents probably feel a sense of shame or guilt for even thinking that it might be best if their child died before they did. Those kinds of thoughts are not selfish in origin but come out of the fear that no one will provide the kind of care for their child that they did. While Linda and Terry are mourning their loss, they are consoled by knowing that they gave Kim their very best for all of their lives—and hers.

Linda wrote me a note after the funeral and gave me permission to share some of it here:

"We've had a lot of support on this journey with Kim. This last year or so has been a struggle so we have to believe she's in a good place now—with other angels. Kimmy impacted so many lives, and we're realizing more than ever before that she was very fortunate to have a network of friends and professionals that supported her (and US!), insuring she have the best life possible."

# Questions for Group Discussion or Self-Reflection

1. If you were to form a microboard for your child, who would be the members?

_____

_____

_____

_____

_____

_____

_____

_____

2. Do you want your child to have their own home? Why or why not?

_____

_____

_____

_____

_____

_____

_____

_____

3. If you were able to set up a home for your child, where would it be located? What kind of home would it be? Would you rent out rooms to others with disabilities?

_____

_____

_____

_____

_____

_____

_____

_____

4. Have you ever thought about your child predeceasing you? Would this be a comfort or a distressing situation for you?

_____

_____

_____

_____

_____

_____

_____

_____

_____

# CHAPTER 8

## *Loving Samantha, Loving All our Children*

In her book, *Loving Samantha*, Karen Jackson shares her journey of experiencing God's love with her daughter who has autism, and I am borrowing her title for this chapter.(1) I connected with Karen after a recommendation from Bill Gaventa, who is a member of the American Association of Intellectual and Developmental Disability.(2) Karen met Bill at a national conference, and he suggested that she contact me regarding her new organization, Faith Inclusion Network of Hampton Roads (FIN).(3) That was five years ago, and currently I am the chair of FIN's board. Karen is the driving force and CEO of FIN, born from her desire to include Samantha in the life of her faith community. Karen, a music teacher in a private school, is married to Scott, and they have two sons in addition to Samantha.

I interviewed Karen in her comfortable living room. Samantha's caregiver was not available that day, so Samantha was watching a *Cat in the Hat* video in the family room. Our time together was limited to the running time of the video. Samantha is Karen and Scott's second child, born when Joseph, their oldest son, was two years old. It was vaginal birth after having a Caesarian with Joseph, who weighed almost ten pounds. Samantha, born in September 1997, was eight pounds, ten ounces. Karen explained that she had gestational diabetes with all three of her pregnancies, causing her to have large babies.

Through her first eighteen months, Samantha's language development was inhibited. Their pediatrician did not share Karen's concern. A neurodevelopmental specialist tested Samantha about a year later and concluded that she was developmentally delayed. However, her gross motor skills were normal. Karen was surprised that Samantha hit those motor developmental milestones earlier than normal.

Karen began to research everywhere she could to learn more about her daughter's condition. This was a trying and difficult period because while she was grieving the loss of the child she hoped Samantha would be, she was also grieving the recent loss of her father, who had died in a car accident. Karen gained new hope when Samantha was enrolled in a special needs preschool at age three, which was a great help. Samantha next attended an early intervention preschool, and she remained in public schools for the rest of her schooling.

Karen and Scott's third child, Jacob, was born in 2002. Karen now had two other children to take with her to Samantha's many appointments. She was trying to meet all of Samantha's many needs in addition to caring for the young boys. Scott encouraged her to stay focused on being "upbeat." He worked two full-time jobs plus extra projects. Karen was exasperated by the lack of one-on-one time with her spouse. She remarked that she now realizes that most couples have to struggle for time alone when they have young children, and perhaps their family was not unusual in that regard. Currently, the biggest issue for Karen is the ongoing challenge of living out their busy family life with a semblance of normality; it never ends.

Samantha is eligible to stay in public school until she's twenty-two, but this may be her last year (she's currently twenty-one). The program she's enrolled in is very structured, but as she is growing older, Samantha would like to have more choices in life. She had a good experience with a day support program the past summer that offered choices of activities, and Karen believes she's ready to transition. Samantha likes a variety of experiences; the day support program provided a routine but with age-appropriate activities that she enjoyed. Karen would like to see Samantha get some kind of part-time work, either as an employee or a volunteer. They've done "a bit" of testing for her skills. Though nonverbal, Samantha enjoys therapeutic recreation programs including bowling, cooking, and getting a manicure. Karen feels that one day, Samantha will be in a long-term residential situation. For the present, having her in a daily program without a family member nearby is a concern for Karen. For the 2016 school year, Samantha and Jacob were in the same high school, and that situation was reassuring to Karen. While she knows that Samantha will develop independence, she is concerned about her vulnerability, as are so many parents of special needs children.

The family has set up a special needs trust, with the parents as guardians (the two sons will later take on this role). Going through the guardianship process set up another round of grieving for Karen. She was remembering when Samantha was age three and Joseph, her older son, was going off to school and was no longer home with her all day. Even though he was young, he was of great help to Karen. Perhaps it was a foreshadowing for Karen of when both boys would be adults and pursing their own lives.

Toward the end of the interview, we moved into deeper issues. Samantha experiences anxiety as well as self-injurious behavior and head-banging. Medications were not helping and even made it worse. Recently, Karen had planned to attend a local event of the Faith Inclusion Network, but Samantha's anxiety was out of control. Karen took her to the emergency room, but it was difficult to get her out of the car. Karen was traumatized by that episode and commented that many parents must experience post-traumatic stress disorder when dealing with similar issues. Samantha now takes medications that keep her behavior from escalating, but Karen is concerned that they are no longer as effective as they once were. Vacations, which Samantha usually enjoys, were not good the past summer. Karen feels helpless when her daughter acts out. She prays a lot and says she could not get through life without faith. She feels she's in "uncharted" waters with Samantha right now. She also feels her faith has grown and cannot imagine not being her mom.

Scott, who is supportive of Karen's efforts with the Faith Inclusion Network, was born and raised a Catholic. She, on the other hand, converted to Catholicism in college, having been raised a United Methodist. As in all families, children grow up and move on. Joseph is in college, and in a few years, Jacob will follow. Scott is very patient with Samantha, but most of the caregiving falls to Karen. She was projecting forward to the coming school year and regular schedules, knowing that she'd soon be dealing with new issues regarding Samantha's needs. Remembering where I was in that phase of the journey several years ago with Chris, I can see myself in Karen, as she contemplates the next steps and deals with the uncertainty of Samantha's future.

While FIN is a unique organization, Karen is not alone; parents of children with special needs often take their own circumstances to the public forum to help others. Parents have always fought to have their children legally included in education, to have good housing, and to have meaningful work and day programs. Parents often form organizations specific to their child's disability and look to each other for support and knowledge; technology has opened the door for more sharing among parents with special needs children, with several types of platforms allowing them to keep in touch.

FIN enables parents to include their children in their faith community. FIN supports and gives encouragement to all faiths through biennial conferences with nationally known speakers, as well as hosting several events a year in Hampton Roads. A new venture has been a partnership to include those with mental illnesses and their families in programming, as these are perhaps the most misunderstood group of people in a church. Their website contains a wealth of information, including links to YouTube videos from the 2015 and 2017 conference. The next big project is a comprehensive resource guide for faith communities to help them to "Accept, Include, Celebrate" (the motto of FIN) those with disabilities.

## Faith Communities and People with Special Needs

I am continually astounded by the stories of parents who encounter ignorance or a lack of compassion when they bring their children with special needs to a service in their faith community. If there is one place that should accept, include, and celebrate these children, it's a house of worship. Parents find that some parishioners are uncomfortable with children (or adults) who make loud noises, sing too loud (or off key), or fidget. The nursery may not want to care for children with special needs, who usually require special care. When approached about having a ministry for children and adults with special needs, some congregations refuse because they're afraid they'll be overwhelmed with too many people who need their help and detract from their other ministries. In actuality, that has never happened, that we know of. The reality is that serving people with special needs brings in their families and their friends, helping with growth in that faith community.

Once when Chris was young, I was asked to leave a church service. The pastor who was giving the sermon was disturbed when Chris woke up from napping on my lap and let out a loud cry (he was startled when he awoke and did not remember where he was at first). When the priest asked me to remove him from the church, I said, "No," and stayed with Chris and his brothers for the remainder of the Mass, with no further incident.

At another church, I asked to place him in a nursery class suitable to his developmental level, but the nursery workers insisted on placing him with other children his age. He couldn't do the same things as those children, but the church was inflexible and wouldn't place him with younger children. Needless to say, things didn't work out there. As my children's father was career Navy and often on deployment, I had no backup for attending church. Sadly, I experienced no understanding or compassion from either faith community. My only recourse was to pay for a babysitter so I could attend church.

Karen's Catholic church provided no proper religious education class for Samantha when she was younger. In addition, Samantha was unable to sit through an entire Mass. Karen and Scott could tag-team each other with Mass schedules and the other children, but Karen wanted her whole family to attend church together. She worked with church staff to accommodate Samantha with a caregiving situation and eventually with religious classes. The entire family was excited when Samantha participated in her Confirmation ceremony. The local newspaper recently carried an article about the church and the encouragement of the pastor to Karen and her family.

My experiences with Chris and church occurred many years before this. At one point, I decided that Chris would receive Communion, contrary to the Catholic tradition that you must take formal classes to receive the sacrament. With no one willing to prepare him, I determined one Sunday that Communion would be a part of his life from that moment. He's never been in a Confirmation class, either.

I joined the United Methodist Church over twenty years ago, and Chris is always welcomed whenever he attends services with me. A number of people come up and talk to us, and many people ask me how he is doing when he is not there. Of course, he is older, and now has no behavioral issues for the most part. I find people in my church very forgiving if he gets a bit impatient or speaks too loud, but that's a rare circumstance.

A faith community can be a significant support to families of special needs children and adults. People look to their faith for support. Many of us wrestle with the concept of the divine purpose in children with disabilities. It may not be compatible with our idea of a loving God to have a child with a disability, and we look to our church for comfort and a way to help make sense of our lives. When a church is unwilling or unable or unaware of the need to give us spiritual guidance and support regarding our child with special needs, we become discouraged. Many families try to find a faith community that welcomes their child, but they often decide to quit attending because it's too difficult. I suspect that there are many families in the latter situation.

In a time when church attendance is decreasing, faith communities could grow by reaching out to families with special needs members, be they adults or children. I was impressed by a church I recently visited. I learned through conversation with a family that the church provided a volunteer to work with their son with ADHD so he would benefit from the children's church experience, while the parents attended the larger church service. The family remains in that church and participates in its other outreach ministries. Charlie is now being prepared for baptism; he is enthusiastic and can tell you all about what God's love means. In this situation, everyone benefits. The family feels supported, and they in turn support the church.

In her book *Different Dream Parenting,* Jolene Philo listed a number of resources to help churches minister to special needs people, including websites and other books. She also incorporated many practical strategies and resources for parents. The emphasis in many chapters is on prayer and scripture, and she provided several monthly prayer guides for many different situations.(4) She is also author of *The Caregiver's Notebook,* which is a detailed organizational tool for those who are caregiving.(5)

In *Dancing with Max,* Emily Colson tells the inspiring story of her faith journey with her son, who has autism. You can also follow her on Facebook or her website (www.emilycolson.com), where she posts updates on Max, who is now twenty-two.(6) Emily speaks at many events, and I was privileged to meet her when she spoke at a FIN event a few years ago. She, Jolene, and Karen are examples of parents who looked to their faith communities for support. They have faith as a priority in raising their special needs children and use their experiences as inspiration to make a difference for others.

# Questions for Group Discussion or Self-Reflection

1. When both parents of an adult with a disability have jobs, how can they work out the home and care duties, especially if there are other siblings?

_____

_____

_____

_____

_____

_____

_____

2. What essential elements are necessary for parents to be a good team in parenting their children?

_____

_____

_____

_____

_____

_____

_____

3. Karen mentions grief regarding Samantha, for the person she would never be. Have you felt this sense of grief and loss in regard to your own child with a disability? What helps you to cope with those feelings?

_____

_____

_____

_____

_____

_____

_____

4. Faith is foundational in Karen's life. Where are you in your own faith journey? Where would you like to be?

_____

_____

_____

_____

_____

_____

_____

# CHAPTER 9

## *Embarking on Adulthood*

*All names in this chapter are fictitious.*

I met with Nancy, a full-time art teacher in a local middle school, at an art museum. We were at the museum because later that evening, she was meeting with parents and students to prepare for an upcoming art trip tour to New York City. Nancy is vibrant and engaging, and her students surely benefit from her positive, energetic personality.

Bernadette is Nancy's twenty-two-year-old daughter. Although Bernadette's parents never married and did not remain in a relationship, they were committed to co-parenting. Unfortunately, Bernadette's father died when she was ten years old. Nancy is now married to Phil, and Bernadette's family includes her stepfather, a thirteen-year-old half-sister, and two stepsisters who do not live with her.

Bernadette is yet another example of a child who was not accurately diagnosed for several years. According to Nancy, when Bernadette was born in 1995, the autism spectrum was narrow (there were few precise characteristics for diagnosis), and Bernadette did not fall into any specific category, although it was clear she had disabilities. At age eight, she was diagnosed with Turner syndrome with mosaicism, which means that some of her cells have the normal amount of chromosomes in her body, and some cells are missing an X chromosome (the distribution of the cells is random, rather like a mosaic picture).(1)(2) Bernadette is currently diagnosed as being on the autism spectrum.

As opposed to when Bernadette was young, a diagnosis of autism now covers a broad range of disability. Autism and autism spectrum disorders (ASDs) are complex neurodevelopmental conditions. Features of ASDs include deficits in communication, undeveloped social skills, and repetitive or restrictive interests and behaviors. Some studies are looking into stem cells and their effectiveness in treating ASDs. No two persons with autism are exactly alike, and there is no one gene responsible for the disability. ASDs are marked by complex gene-environmental interactions.(3)

Bernadette completed public school at age twenty-one; she was one of a dozen public school students with special needs chosen to be in a unique project at a regional medical center. In this job training program, Bernadette learned a new task every twelve weeks, acquiring a variety of skills. The program also enrolled her into the Department of Aging and Rehabilitative Services (DARS), which provided her with a job coach.(4) Bernadette now works as a bagger at a large grocery store and also does some custodial work. She loves her job because she loves to be around people. Her stepfather usually picks her up from work, but if he's late, she uses the Uber app on her phone to get a ride home. She participates in many Special Olympics activities and enjoys vacations with her mother and half-sister, including cruises and a trip to the Grand Canyon.

Bernadette is fortunate to have a job; the majority of adults with disabilities are either unemployed or underemployed. The program she took part in was a pathway to meaningful employment, resulting economic, social, and life satisfaction benefits.(5) Unfortunately, too few schools have such an opportunity. Bernadette has many talents, including being able to remember dates. During the interview, Nancy couldn't recall the year Bernadette's father died; she texted her daughter to get the date, and she immediately replied, "2005." Nancy says that she remembers everything.

Nancy applied for a Medicaid waiver for Bernadette, but there were paperwork errors on the first try, and they are reapplying. She is considering establishing an ABLE account for Bernadette.(6) Nancy would like to have an aide in the home for Bernadette, even though her younger daughter is a big help. To provide for Bernadette's future, Nancy has established a trust funded by insurance policies. If a situation arises where Nancy can no longer care for Bernadette, she would live with Nancy's mother, who is in her seventies, or with Nancy's cousin, who is close to Nancy's age. However, Nancy said she feels that she and Bernadette will be "two little old ladies" living out their lives together.

When asked about the role of faith in raising Bernadette, Nancy replied that faith made a "huge impact" in both of their lives. Bernadette belonged to Young Life for a while but said she doesn't really like attending Church services. (7) Their current church attendance is sporadic, partially because it is a new church for them, and they don't know many people. They both watch Joel Osteen and Joyce Meyer on TV. Nancy thinks that Bernadette would prefer a church class rather than attending a service. If such a class were available, she feels they would attend church more.

Phil works long hours in the medical field. Nancy reports that they've had disagreements about some issues in parenting Bernadette. The couple has been to three marriage counselors, but they've been unable to resolve the situation.

## Stresses on Parents

Each chapter in this book describes a multitude of stressors parents experience by having a child (now an adult) with a disability. Some couples remained together; some did not. I have not yet found anything in the research literature that defines which factors are present when couples with a special needs child stay together and what causes the demise of relationships that do not last.

Although there are no accurate data available regarding marital problems among parents of special needs children, stress connected with raising a child with a disability is more the norm than not. Seth Ayers wrote on his website about his son who has special needs, who he adopted at age two.(8) Ayers noted that parents may resent their child or feel exhaustion, frustration, or depression. Parents may also experience a negative influence on their own mental health, and in some cases, there may be stress equivalent to experiencing post-traumatic stress disorder, as might be experienced in combat. That stress can be so great as to shorten a parent's life by nine to twelve years.(9)

Ayers also addressed the extra duties of parents with special needs children, including the "thousands of hours" spent by parents in teaching the child self-care. I can verify those hours from my experience with Chris. I spent two years teaching him a routine to follow when he arrived home from school. The pattern was: Come in the door, hang up your coat, use the bathroom and wash your hands, get your snack, and then watch your favorite shows: *Sesame Street, Mister Rogers' Neighborhood,* and *Electric Company.* Before he learned the routine, there was chaos every day because he was upset at having to get off his beloved yellow school bus and come into the house. I don't remember how many hours we spent together for that routine. However, I do know that the payoff was worth the effort, as Chris then independently took care of himself after school every day. My home office was directly below Chris's second-floor bedroom, and the songs from all those shows played above me the year I worked on my doctoral dissertation. It was a beautiful day in the neighborhood.

# Questions for Group Discussion or Self-Reflection

1.  Bernadette was fortunate to be in a pregraduation program that gave her some training and skills, resulting in a job she enjoys. Are there any such programs in your area?

_____

_____

_____

_____

_____

_____

_____

_____

_____

_____

2.  Bernadette seems to have few peer contacts. As she grows older, do you see this as being more of a problem or less of a problem?

_____

_____

_____

_____

_____

_____

_____

_____

_____

_____

_____

3.  What might be done to encourage Bernadette to participate in her faith community? How could Nancy make her pastor aware of the kinds of needs Bernadette has, such as a church class?

_____

_____

_____

_____

_____

_____

_____

_____

_____

## CHAPTER 10

# The Rabbi's Daughter

I met with Rebecca for lunch in a restaurant. We've known each other for several years, but we never had an opportunity to sit down and share stories because we were always working at events or in formal meetings together. Because she recently retired from her teaching career, we had time for a long and enjoyable lunch. Right away, Rebecca wanted to make sure that I was not asking her for the "official Jewish position" on disability. I assured her that I was not, and the interview began.

Rebecca led off with this statement: "Annoyances at Hailey are more annoying now that I have time," referring to her being at home more now that she's no longer working. She then admitted that "Hailey controls my buttons. She has me on speed-dial." It was apparent that Rebecca was somewhat frustrated with being Hailey's primary caregiver.

Hailey is the eldest of Rebecca's three children. She and her husband, a rabbi, also have two younger sons. Hailey was born in June 1981 at eight pounds, five ounces, after a normal pregnancy but a difficult delivery. When Rebecca expressed concern to the pediatrician about Hailey's developmental delays, such as not walking until past two years old, he blamed the birth situation. After a referral to a neurologist, Hailey was diagnosed at age two and a half with low-tone cerebral palsy. At age three, Hailey was enrolled in special education classes and had an Individualized Educational Plan (IEP). She continued her education at a private school for children with special needs, but Rebecca didn't know what her diploma signified as far as skills obtained or abilities developed.

In 1990, two months before her ninth birthday, and memorable for Rebecca because it was Passover, Hailey was diagnosed with Leigh's disease, a degenerative disorder.(1) The diagnosis was reached following nine days in the hospital after having "ragged" breathing in the pediatrician's office. When she returned home from the hospital, Rebecca said that it took six months for her to be able to sit up again. According to Rebecca and the neurologist (who has treated her annually since that year), Hailey is one of the few people in this world with this condition who have reached her age and is currently medically stable. However, a few months ago, Hailey experienced loss of feeling in her legs, which led to her falling often. She is once again stable.

Hailey travels back and forth to her volunteer job using Handi-Ride transportation and communicates with Rebecca by texting on her cell phone when she's away from home. She functions on the level of a third or fourth grader and is able to read books such as those in the *Diary of a Wimpy Kid* series; she also does crafts at home. The main problem for Rebecca is that she's not sure what Hailey actually understands. She cannot distinguish if her daughter's behaviors are due to the disability or if she's just being resistant. For example, Hailey will ask members of the congregation to tie her shoes for her when Rebecca knows that she can do this for herself. She wonders if these behaviors are aimed at attention-getting. Rebecca feels that the congregation "panders" to her.

However, Hailey has a sweet and kind nature and loves the congregation members, and they all love her. For example, they take her to the movies, and Hailey calls people to wish them well. She remembers others' birthdays by sending cards but ignores her parents' birthdays, puzzling Rebecca and leading her to believe that Hailey is manipulating and taking advantage of people. Yet she also feels that Hailey wants independence and is always testing the boundaries. For now, Rebecca contents herself with knowing that the synagogue is Hailey's community, and she is thriving in it.

Rebecca always assumed that Hailey would predecease her parents, given her diagnosis, but now that she's medically stable, she looks at things in a different way and realizes she needs to learn more about current and future services for her daughter. We discussed a number of resources that might be helpful to the family. Rebecca felt uninformed because she has no case worker for Hailey and has had no outside guidance on what steps to take next.

When asked what keeps her going, Rebecca's immediate reply was, "Necessity." She specified a disclaimer that although she's the wife of a rabbi, she didn't believe that Hailey's disability was the result of God's will, nor that she and her husband were chosen to have a child with a disability. She said that Hailey defines a great part of who she is and that she cannot imagine life without being responsible for her. She used a metaphor to describe her life with her daughter: "The trees are the daily annoyances of living with Hailey, and the forest is the larger picture." Her closing comment was, "Who would have thought that Hailey would turn out to be as capable as she is?"

## Inclusion in the Jewish Community

Rebecca did not want to be the expert on a Jewish perspective of disability, so I turned to my friend, Shelly Christensen, the founder and executive director of Inclusion Innovations, who describes herself as a disability, inclusion, and belonging specialist.(2) Shelly explained that the framework for a theology of disability for Judaism is in two concepts based on scripture. The first is Genesis 1:26: "And God said, Let us make man in our image, after our likeness." Because we are created in God's image, we should treat each other accordingly, Shelly explained. She added to this verse the concept of *Ahavat Yisrael*, loving people as you love yourself, treating all people with love and kindness (but not patronizing them, which is demeaning). She further built on this concept by discussing Rabbi Menachem Mendel Schneerson, the seventh Lubavitcher Rebbe, who died in 1994. He was known as the inspirational and pragmatic leader of the worldwide Jewish Chabad-Lubavitch movement, which taught that we treat others as they want to be treated and not how we want to treat them. (3) The important idea is building a relationship with people, not just doing good for someone. Shelly gave examples of good things congregations do, such as bringing people with disabilities to services for Chanukah, but they may not pay attention to them other times of the year. In other words, they don't build relationships with their guests. Another example is of a young person celebrating a bar or bat mitzvah and engaging in some kind of activity with a person with a disability because they needed a project. They may have made the person merely a project and not contributed to developing a sense of belonging for that person in the congregation.

The second scriptural reference is Deuteronomy 29:10-15:

> Ye stand this day all of you before the LORD your God; your captains of your tribes, your elders, and your officers, with all the men of Israel, Your little ones, your wives, and thy stranger that is in thy camp, from the hewer of thy wood unto the drawer of thy water: That thou shouldest enter into covenant with the LORD thy God, and into his oath, which the LORD thy God maketh with thee this day: That he may establish thee today for a people unto himself, and that he may be unto thee a God, as he hath said unto thee, and as he hath sworn unto thy fathers, to Abraham, to Isaac, and to Jacob. Neither with you only do I make this covenant and this oath; But with him that standeth here with us this day before the LORD our God, and also with him that is not here with us this day.

Shelly referred to this passage as a clear indication of the intent of God to have all people, no matter their status, included in the covenant and going forward to the Promised Land. Also, in the beginning of Deuteronomy 30, Moses tells the people to take all the things they've been told in their hearts and heed the commands with all of their heart and soul. This, Shelly said, shows that everyone has access to the heart and soul of Judaism, which is the Torah.

The story of Moses illustrates how God has a place for everyone. God called Moses to be the greatest leader of the Jewish people, yet Moses, who had a speech disorder, argued with God because he did not want to speak to Pharaoh. God provided that his brother Aaron would be his voice, thereby making the first recorded accommodation for a person with a disability, according to Shelly. The story shows how we are all God's partners, disability or not. We each have strengths and weaknesses, but we each have a uniqueness—*neshama*—the soul, which carries our gifts to be used to make the world a better place.

We spoke of modern Judaism and the application of these scriptures to current congregational life. Jewish congregations have inclusion committees, but Shelly feels that more can be done. Jewish Disability Awareness Month (JDAIM) is recognized every February in synagogues and Jewish communities around the world. In the ten years since its inception, JDAIM has grown from four communities to become a worldwide recognition that synagogues and communities have an obligation to support people with disabilities in Jewish life, with many activities taking place.(4)

Shelly is encouraged by the fact that many more parents are now feeling that their child is understood in the congregation and in Sunday school. However, she remains concerned about people in congregations she calls "gatekeepers," those persons who do not understand that one should not have to fit into an existing program, but that congregations need to look at each individual's needs and desires, and then accommodate them as fully as possible. The goal should be to support people to achieve their best selves. From Shelly's definition, it would seem that Hailey has just that type of supportive congregation.

# Questions for Group Discussion or Self-Reflection

1.  Do you think that many parents are similar to Rebecca, who do not want to be an unofficial spokesperson for their particular faith denomination?

   _____

   _____

   _____

   _____

   _____

   _____

   _____

   _____

2.  Is Hailey being coddled by her congregation, or is this a positive situation where social needs are being met?

   _____

   _____

   _____

   _____

   _____

   _____

   _____

   _____

3. When a parent retires, do responsibilities of caregiving for the adult with disabilities increase? Why or why not?

_____

_____

_____

_____

_____

_____

_____

_____

4. Retirement implies time to do things on one's own without having to report to a job every day. How might having Hailey in the home prevent Rebecca from following her own desires?

_____

_____

_____

_____

_____

_____

_____

_____

_____

CHAPTER 11

# Building on Faith, Hope, and Love

The story of my friend, Hugh Harris, a retired Methodist minister, and his brother Paul, who had cerebral palsy (CP), is an inspiring tale of how a family came together to support their adult with special needs in a unique way. Although his parents have passed on, Hugh gave me their perspective as well as his own to include here.

Paul Robert Harris was born in 1943, when Hugh was six, and lived until 1989. The family also had two other children, a boy and a girl. Hugh, being the eldest, learned caregiving for Paul, including simple cooking. He remained in this role until he joined the army and left home. At that point, the youngest brother, Jim, twelve years younger, stepped into Hugh's role of being a helper. Hugh's sister, known as Sissy, was born with a hole in her heart, had a heart murmur, and required special care for a time. She lived until sixty-two, dying after hitting her head on the floor during a diabetic seizure.

Hugh has only sketchy memories of Paul's early days. Not much about Paul's condition was discussed in the home, but he does remember that his brother was not meeting developmental milestones. A pediatrician diagnosed him at six months with spastic paralysis and advised his parents to put Paul in a home, forget about him, and go on with their lives. The Harris family ignored that advice, as did everyone else I interviewed for this book. Paul was a large part of Hugh's life. He told me that Paul could not walk, even with braces, so Hugh would put his brother's feet on his, hold on to him, and walk him around the yard.

When Hugh's mother, Mary Ellen (nee Townsend), was pregnant with Jim, her obstetrician was knowledgeable about the Rh factor, having worked in a maternity hospital in World War II. The Rh factor caused Paul's CP, and Mary Ellen was fearful of the outcome of this pregnancy. Because she had to have total bed rest for several weeks, Hugh and his sister stayed with their grandparents during that time; they placed Paul in a convalescent home until several weeks after Jim's birth, the only time Paul was away from his family.

For a time, Paul's parents were part of a parents' group who wanted to found a CP center. Apparently, others were involved in setting criteria for that center because Paul did not qualify to be enrolled; he did not meet the requirement of being able to feed himself. Subsequently, the Harrises formed a CP support group in their home with several other parents. They later had meetings in a Methodist church in Cincinnati; this congregation was of great support to the family for a number of years.

Mary Ellen periodically took Paul by train to a doctor in Cockeysville, Maryland. On one of those medical trips, the entire Harris family decided to travel by car; they stopped overnight in the Shenandoah Valley of Virginia. Hugh's parents were drawn to the valley and decided to move the family there. They eventually relocated to Keezeltown, Virginia, which Hugh says was the best thing that ever happened to him. He learned a lot of life lessons about being a newcomer to an area, including being new in a school, and subsequently had the experience of growing up in both the city and the country.

For Hugh's parents, Paul was a uniting factor. Hugh describes his father (Hugh Sr.) as a "loving enabler" for Paul. He recalled him building Paul a special chair and other furniture items and said he was always working and advocating for his son. Because there was no placement for Paul in Virginia after he completed public schooling, his parents built the Community of Hope (COHOPE), a residential school that was completed in 1972 after ten years of fund-raising, construction, and licensing. The primary funding had been through fund-raising drives, but several people left donations for the facility in their wills. Over the years, there were a few residential students, but the school served mostly day students from the local area. Paul's parents worked at COHOPE for all of the years it existed, but they never took a salary. Between the time that Paul's public school ended and the completion of COHOPE, Mary Ellen provided daily activities for Paul, sending off for learning material and also creating lessons and activities on her own.

Mary Ellen and another staff member could understand Paul's speech, and they lovingly wrote out his thoughts and added simple illustrations to create a handwritten book.(1) Hugh related that if the women did not get a word correctly, Paul would say, "No," until they said the right word, a painstaking process. Paul, however, was the sole author. There's a picture of Paul in the introduction to the book. Below the picture are Mary Ellen's words: "It is his wish and mine that you will be uplifted, encouraged in your daily life and, as you journey through these pages, find the joy of a closer walk with God." Paul dedicated the book to his mother. The following is one of his poems.

*I Wonder*

Why do people look so sad when I am happy?

Why do we all look down at ourselves?

Because we do not know to look up at the heavens.

I look up in the heavens and I see the Lord in the blue sky,

And all the people are looking down at themselves,

when I am looking up in heaven.

Five days before he died, Paul told his mother that he was going on a trip. As Hugh recounted, at 7:30 on the morning of Paul's death, Hugh saw a vision of Paul standing at the foot of his bed and heard him saying, "I'm all right." Within seconds, Hugh had a phone call telling him that Paul had died. Hugh remembered that Mary Ellen felt she was "called" to be Paul's mother, but I believe that Hugh was also called to be Paul's big brother.

This story of a family that created a world for their son with a disability is inspiring. So many schools, groups, programs, and laws came into being because of those dedicated parents who would not give up on their children with disabilities and wanted a better life for them. I find that although we now have federal and state laws for the education of all children, it is still parents and siblings who are making a difference in the lives of their family members, benefitting many others in the process.

Not many people recognize that when programs and accommodations are made for people with disabilities, we all benefit. Curb cuts and automatic doors that accommodate physically handicapped people benefit all of us. If you are pushing a stroller, for example, or carrying items with full arms into a building, you appreciate these modifications. Laws that provide for education of children with disabilities have increased awareness of the wide spectrum of children and adults with special needs.

Thank you to those parents who have gone before me and pushed open the doors wide enough so that when my son needed a school, there was one for him. Thank you to universities for educating teachers to focus on special needs. Thank you to localities for expanding early childhood education and in-home care and Medicaid waivers, none of which would have happened without families like the Harrises. Parents and siblings of adults with disabilities cannot rest on these accomplishments. We are all called upon to remain vocal and watchful, protecting and advocating for those who cannot speak for themselves.(2)

# Questions for Group Discussion or Self-Reflection

1.  What is different today from fifty years ago, when Paul's parents founded a post-high school program for him and others?

   _____

   _____

   _____

   _____

   _____

   _____

   _____

   _____

2.  What kinds of regulations would they have to follow today that may not have been in place back then?

   _____

   _____

   _____

   _____

   _____

   _____

   _____

3. Do we as parents have more or less control over what we want for our children with special needs?

_____

_____

_____

_____

_____

_____

_____

_____

4. Are opportunities today better or worse than they were in Paul's lifetime?

_____

_____

_____

_____

_____

_____

_____

_____

_____

## CHAPTER 12

# For Jenny (1969–2003)

The lives of my son Chris and Jenny intersected through their years at school. Jenny was a few years behind Chris in school, but they traveled the same paths for preschool and grade school. Jenny's mom, Berny, and I served on some committees together, but the interview for this book was my first chance to hear the entire story of Jenny's life. I am grateful for the opportunity to learn in detail about this family and the loving care they provided for their daughter.

Jenny was born in January 1969, a healthy baby at eight pounds. According to Berny, she seemed more quiet and passive than her other two babies, also girls. When Jenny was six months old, Berny mentioned Jenny's lack of activity to her pediatrician, who brushed off her concerns. At seven months, Jenny sat up, and at nine months, she would crawl, but slowly and lethargically. One day when she was eleven months old, she was standing in her crib and crying, and Berny realized that she didn't know how to sit down.

When Jenny was a year old, she had an ear infection, and at the same time, Duncan, her father, noticed that she had tremors in her hands. He and Berny took Jenny to a hospital out of state, where she stayed for a month, undergoing a variety of tests. Fortunately, there was a regular bed in Jenny's room, so Berny remained with her during that time. She recalls that hectic month, with the girls in primary school and needing care, and

Duncan working as a psychiatrist. Friends and family helped, and Duncan gave Berny a break by staying at the hospital on weekends. The diagnosis was Leigh's disease, a progressive neurological disorder, and the projection was that Jenny would not live past four years old, as she was regressing developmentally and getting weaker.

At age two, Jenny was in a clinical study in Washington DC. However, for Jenny to be enrolled, Berny had to be part of the control group in order to stay with her, so mother and daughter underwent the same testing. Later, a doctor came to their home to collect skin samples and draw blood in order to find a proper treatment for Jenny. Berny said that they were "in a frenzy" to find treatment. They gave her lipoic acid shots daily and treated her for thiamine deficiency, which turned her skin yellow. After three months with no improvement, Berny and Duncan decided to stop the treatments.

Jenny needed assistive medical equipment to sit upright for feeding, playing, and socializing. At that time, there was a scarcity of good equipment available for children. A friend built a table that surrounded Jenny so she could sit up and have toys nearby to stimulate her. Her parents found a travel wheelchair, but finding an appropriate car seat was difficult. Before the safety seats we use today existed, car seats for children did not offer adequate physical support.

In 1974, Jenny attended half-day kindergarten, travelling to a self-contained special education school in a station wagon. The next year, she rode in a regular school bus for full-day school, but because handicapped buses were not yet standard in the school system, she rode in her travel wheelchair. In 1989, her former school closed, and she attended school at a new wing of the local public high school. Berny noted that certain school personnel made an immense difference in Jenny's life: the school nurse, the speech therapist, and the physical therapist. Jenny graduated in 1991 with a certificate of attendance. After high school, she attended a day support program.

Throughout her school years and beyond, Jenny had many health crises. When she was seventeen, her laryngeal muscles collapsed, and she needed an emergency tracheotomy. The family now had to learn about tracheotomy care. For example, Jenny started eating a lot more than usual, but Berny didn't know why. Eventually, she learned that Jennifer was hungry because she was aspirating food; it was not going into her stomach. Jenny's movement disorder became worse; the constant motion was so strong that she could dislodge her tube, which happened during her sister's wedding. This five-foot-tall redhead with a maximum weight of sixty pounds could generate a lot of power. Berny recalled sitting in the back pew of the church during the wedding, constantly adjusting the tube.

In the late 1990s, Jenny developed a fingernail fungus. The doctor gave her a prescription but it didn't work, so he doubled the dose. However, since she weighed only sixty pounds, her body couldn't tolerate the higher dose, and she became very ill. She was vomiting and could not eat. The family was on vacation in Pennsylvania and drove her to the nearest hospital. They diagnosed her with pancreatitis, so they decided to return home immediately. Duncan took the seats out of their van and made a padded bed for Jenny in the back. They gave her valium to keep her still because with her constant motion, she could injure herself in the van. The family traveled back from vacation with Jenny wearing an IV bag and a catheter; they took her straight to the hospital near their home.

At the hospital, she had a GI tube and a nasogastric tube inserted; there was blood in the GI tube, so Jenny underwent surgery for a bleeding ulcer. Part of her stomach was removed. Ever since that incident, she's had gastric problems. Berny could not stay overnight in the hospital with her because there was nowhere for her to sleep. During her stay, and due to her movement disorder, Jenny broke her foot because she had wedged it into the bed but could not stop moving her foot. After the surgery, the doctors recommended feeding her by GI tube, but Berny refused because food was one of Jenny's greatest pleasures, and her parents didn't want to deny her that.

Jenny had another hospitalization in the late 1990s. Her parents were in New York for their grandson's first birthday party. Jenny had an excellent caregiver, who was driving them both to the movies when they were rear-ended by another car. The EMTs strapped Jenny to a body board and put her in a hospital bed on the board, but unfortunately, they left her there for fourteen hours. With her movement disorder, she had rubbed the skin off her back. It took ten months for the coccyx bedsore to heal, with the help of a wound specialist. Berny and Duncan met with the hospital, not to exact any kind of retribution, but to let them know what had happened, hoping to prevent a similar experience from occurring to anyone else.

Families keep changing as children grow and move on with their lives. In addition to Jenny's story, this family's journey also includes Berny's miscarriage and the later adoption of a baby boy. Berny often wondered over the years if the son she lost would have had the same disabilities as Jenny.

Berny worked in Duncan's office through the 1990s, which meant a caregiver was needed for the hours when Jenny was not in day support. The family hired a number of caregivers over the years, and as can happen, not everyone was suitable. However, they finally found a wonderful and capable person who helped with Jenny until her death. They also outfitted the house in a unique way to properly care for their daughter. Berny hired a decorator who specialized in boats and transformed a large closet into a bed and changing station. On the right side of the closet is a berth such as you would find in a boat but with padded, robin's-egg-blue walls and a movable padded bed railing. On the other side is a cushioned changing table with the same blue padded walls and a sink that could be used to shampoo her beautiful red hair. They also built an adjoining suite onto their house for a caregiver and put in a shower that could accommodate Jenny. Berny was grateful that she and Duncan could afford these changes for Jenny as well as whatever services she needed. She expressed concern for families who had children with special needs who were unable to afford these amenities.

As Jenny grew older, it became increasingly difficult to keep her upright. Although her body was small, her head was of normal adult size and was heavy for her body to support. They had to keep her feet and arms restrained so she didn't injure herself. As her parents were also growing older, it became harder for them to manage her. In 2002, they decided to move her to the first intermediate care facility in their area. They customized her room there, despite facing opposition from the board who ran the nonprofit. They put in running water and added cushioning around her bed, as they had done in their home. They added a baby monitor in her room because the rules stipulated that bedroom doors had to be closed at night, and they were concerned that she might need care during the night.

After moving to her new residence, Jenny often visited at home on

Sundays. A routine was established that staff would take her to church, and then Duncan and Berny would bring her home from church for the day and return her in the evening to the ICF. On one Sunday visit, Berny noticed that Jenny looked as though she was dozing but soon realized that she wasn't breathing. She and Duncan attempted CPR and took her to the nearby hospital, but nothing could be done. Berny was grateful that Jenny died at home, with her family. The cause of death was heart arrhythmia, one of the side effects of Vioxx, a drug Jenny had taken for a year to help with her many aches and pains (the drug was removed from the US market in 2004).

After Jenny died, her family donated her organs so they could be used by others. They sent her brain to a university hospital for an autopsy, but there was no sign of Leigh's disorder, which was surprising news. The family learned that what they thought was Leigh's disease was most likely a biochemical imbalance.

Berny recalls Jenny's life positively. She said that she and Duncan wanted her to have as normal a life as possible. They traveled with her and made sure she had good experiences. On one occasion, Duncan carried her to the top of a historic lighthouse, and another day, he took her into the ocean. Berny saw them get hit by a wave that knocked them over, and Jenny was delighted.

Their two daughters were supportive and helpful whenever they could be. They had support from their church, which allowed Jenny to remain in the second grade Sunday school class, even after she was no longer in that age range. They later switched to another church closer to home, where Jenny was also accepted.

As most parents who have children with special needs do, Berny asked herself, "Why?" but she said she quickly moved on to, "Why not?" She rejects the idea that parents are selected by God because of their own qualities to parent such a child. She has come to rely on trusting God and taking each day as it comes. She said that after Jenny died, while the whole family was sad, she and Duncan also experienced relief after all the years of caregiving. They were free now to enjoy retirement without the constant worry and concern for Jenny.

Berny was honored that a local ICF facility was named "Jenny's Place" in her memory.

# Questions for Discussion or Self-Reflection

1. Children with both medical and intellectual development issues present increased challenges. How did these parents manage the medical needs of their children?

_____

_____

_____

_____

_____

_____

_____

_____

2. Do you think Jenny lived as long as she did because her parents had the medical knowledge to care for her?

_____

_____

_____

_____

_____

_____

_____

_____

_____

_____

3. These parents chose to keep their child at home with a caregiver for a long time. Other parents may not be able to do so if their child is so medically involved. How can a congregation support a family who chooses a care setting out of the home?

_____

_____

_____

_____

_____

_____

_____

_____

_____

_____

# CHAPTER 13

## College Bound

*All names in this chapter are fictitious.*

Nadia is a health care professional and a divorced mom of two sons. Her elder son, Thomas, has Duchenne muscular dystrophy (DMD), and her second son, William, is in high school. Thomas recently graduated from high school and takes classes at a local community college. According to the Muscular Dystrophy Association, one person in five thousand in the United States has either DMD or Becker's MD (a milder form). DMD is one of nine forms of muscular dystrophy, characterized by progressive muscular deterioration and weakness.(1)

Thomas was born in April 1998 and weighed seven pounds, eight ounces after a pregnancy complicated by gestational diabetes. As months went on, Nadia noticed that Thomas was not reaching normal developmental milestones; he did not crawl at the expected age and did not walk until age two. When she mentioned these delays to her pediatrician, he was not concerned. At age three, Thomas could not run. Nadia again brought this delay to the pediatrician's attention, who then referred him to a specialist. After a blood test, Thomas was diagnosed with DMD. Nadia took him to a local Muscular Dystrophy Association (MDA) free clinic but did not find sufficient help there. A group of parents, including Nadia, were instrumental in having the clinic relocated to a local children's hospital, and a better level of care ensued.

Later, with blood drawn from Thomas and his parents at the Baltimore Duchenne Care Clinic, genetic testing showed that Nadia, now seven months' pregnant with William, was a carrier of the gene for DMD. William had a 50 percent chance of also having DMD. William was born in 2001 but showed no signs of DMD, to Nadia's great relief.

Once diagnosed, Thomas received occupational therapy and physical therapy services; he began talking when he was four years old. As he grew older, new medical concerns developed, and there were some additional developmental delays. All the while, Nadia brought Thomas to see many doctors in several specialties, including cardiology, pulmonology, physiology, neurology, and ophthalmology.

Thomas attended public school for all of his schooling, from prekindergarten to graduation from high school. Although he had a period of adjustment in the early grades, he adapted well as he progressed through school. In middle school, he was a member of the National Junior Honor Society, and he had good grades in high school. While in high school, he developed a new app for a game that people paid a fee to play. Thomas's advancing school progress was in contrast to his declining physical issues. By the end of seventh grade, at age thirteen, he had to use a wheelchair for mobility, even though he was still walking part of the time. He now uses the wheelchair all of the time.

Thomas participated in the youth group in his church and was part of the Confirmation class. He was able to participate in some trips because the youth director provided a wheelchair-accessible van to transport him. However, when Thomas attends church, his wheelchair sits in the aisle because there's no other place for it. As I put myself in his situation, I can only imagine how it feels to be so obviously different without the additional onus of being highly visible in a church service. Although many churches offer accessibility, such as ramps and elevators, placement for people in wheelchairs is not always optimum. A solution for inclusion of wheelchairs in churches could be artfully placed pew cuts, or as my church did recently, replace some pews with movable chairs, eliminating having to put a wheelchair in an aisle.

Thomas presently is enjoying life as a student at a community college.

His goal is to complete an associate's degree in computer science and transfer to a four-year university to major in that field. Being a college student has brought some new challenges to Thomas. He relies on an aide for personal care and transportation. One day, the aide didn't show up, and he couldn't be present at class to physically turn in a paper. Unfortunately, the teacher allowed no other options for him, such as sending in the paper by email, and so he received a zero for the paper. Thomas was naturally upset. Despite having a grade of C in the course, he was on the Dean's List that term. At present, Nadia is the backup plan for when an aide is a no-show, but she cannot always provide what he needs because of her job.

Thomas tries to be as independent as possible by being in charge of his prescriptions and going grocery shopping. Another facet of his independence is that he decided not to go to visit his father every other weekend, as he once did. One reason is that the ramp at his father's house isn't up to code. Another is a heavy load of traveling, due to being in a clinical trial program for DMD, which began after Thomas began losing the ability to use his arms. Nadia drives him to Baltimore once a month, and three times a month, they drive to Moyock, North Carolina, which is closer to their home. Although it's a lot of driving, it's better than the previous schedule, which meant driving round-trip to Baltimore and back every Tuesday for over a year, over four hundred miles each time. The drug has stopped his loss of mobility but hasn't restored his arm strength. The drug now has FDA approval, but he remains in a clinical trial until his health insurance approves him to have the drug at home.

When asked what keeps her going, Nadia replied that the MDA parent group has been a big help, and so has her faith. She was not a Christian when Thomas was diagnosed, and she calls it a "dark time" in her life. After William was born, she started attending church. She and the boys' father divorced when Thomas was in seventh grade.

Nadia is concerned about Thomas's future on many levels, including medical, social, and economic, but she takes things as they arise, one day at a time. Attending William's band competitions and taking her sons on nonmedical vacations keeps her involved and busy with her family. She is also close to her own parents, who live out of state, and there are regular back-and-forth visits, giving Nadia strong support. She has many unanswered questions, such as about Thomas's ability to be gainfully employed in the future, as well as ongoing health concerns. However, this family remains positive in outlook and lives life to the fullest extent.

## Accommodations in Higher Education

Thomas's inability to submit his paper to his teacher in person and receiving a zero grade seems archaic in this time of technology with so many institutions (including Thomas's) teaching courses online. It is important for students with disabilities in any postsecondary institution to know their rights and responsibilities to have the best possible educational experience. Programs are not obliged to change courses or curricula, but they must, by law, provide reasonable accommodations as needed by the student.(2)

Students must request an accommodation for a disability from the office of the college or university specified for that function. The student must initiate the process, and then the institution decides on whether the accommodation is reasonable, using provisions of Section 504 of the Rehabilitation Act of 1973 as a guideline. However, not all requests can be granted because some needs are not covered by the law, such as personal care. A disability has to have a specific diagnosis and can range from having a learning disability to a need for physical access. Thomas was granted his requests to have an aide in the classroom and to be late to class, but he didn't specifically ask to be able to submit papers electronically, quite likely because he didn't think he'd ever need to do so. It's impossible to predict all the situations where accommodations will be needed. For each student, the process is highly individualized.(3)

When I was an academic dean in charge of a large program, I worked with students who requested accommodations, so I am familiar with the process. Schools have limited resources, and adaptations had to be made within my annual budget. However, we could do many things. We often allowed students with ADHD to take tests separately, in case they needed more time to complete the test. Also, we could print only one test question per page, if needed. We allowed longer times to take tests. We made large-print pages for tests for students with visual problems. These were all easy alterations. With the rise of computers, more adaptations are available using online resources.

What we could not do was to approve changes for students who stated they had learning problems but did not produce a written medical diagnosis. Accommodations are generally not for temporary problems, like getting the flu or having a broken leg. In those kinds of cases, one would hope for compassionate teachers who would work out a reasonable solution with their students. The strict standards are to prevent abuse of the law.

# Questions for Group Discussion or Self-Reflection

1. Being a single mom with a full-time job is a daunting task for anyone, but more so when a child has a disability. What strengths did you see in Nadia as head of her household?

_____

_____

_____

_____

_____

_____

_____

2. As Thomas grew older, he became more disabled physically, and at the same time, Nadia did not have the physical strength to care for him alone. What are the advantages and disadvantages of having a personal aide in the home?

_____

_____

_____

_____

_____

_____

_____

3. Do you think people with visible disabilities have a more difficult time finding employment than someone with no apparent disability? Do you know anyone with disabilities who is underemployed or unable to find work? Are you concerned that your own child will have employment difficulties?

_____

_____

_____

_____

_____

_____

_____

4. What can schools (high school and college) do to facilitate employability of their graduates? What role do parents have in moving employability forward?

_____

_____

_____

_____

_____

_____

_____

_____

## CHAPTER 14

# *Fiercely Independent*

*All names in this chapter are fictitious.*

I met Katie, a business owner, for the first time on the day of the interview. I called her upon the recommendation of a mutual friend, and she graciously accepted my request to participate in this project. In December 1968, Katie's son, Bart, the first of her three children, was born two months premature, weighing five pounds. Bart remained in the hospital for three weeks, and when Katie, nineteen at the time, asked about possible developmental problems, the pediatrician told her that "preemies are delayed but they catch up." However, by the time of Bart's first birthday, he had not caught up. Another doctor told her at that time that Bart was severely disabled and should be placed in an institution. Katie, who was at the doctor's office alone, was emotionally devastated and overwhelmed at hearing this diagnosis. She was so shattered by this news, she doesn't remember how she managed to carry Bart out of the office and get into the car.

Katie's next step was to learn more about Bart's problems. The family was living in Pennsylvania at the time, and Bart was tested at a hospital there over a period of six months. At the conclusion of the testing, Katie received the same advice the first doctor had given her: to put Bart into an institution before she became attached to him. I was given that same recommendation, as were so many other parents of that era. Fortunately, institutionalization of babies is no longer standard medical advice. Katie and I wondered how many parents were told to place their babies with intellectual disabilities out of the home, and how many followed through.

When Katie told me about Bart's current situation, I was somewhat amazed that he has become so independent. He has cerebral palsy and is essentially a quadriplegic. He has problems with gross motor skills (large muscle movement), but his fine motor skills are "okay," according to Katie. He is legally blind but has excellent verbal skills. Katie attributes his verbal facility to his being placed in special education classes with children with severe disabilities whose language skills were less than Bart's. Because he did not get responses from his classmates, he sought out his teachers and aides for conversation and so developed his verbal competence.

Katie stated that she spent a lot of time and effort finding appropriate schooling and transportation for Bart, but the results were not always ideal. Every school day of his early years, she had to first lift him onto the school bus, load the wheelchair in, and then repeat the process in reverse when he came home. Katie said that her being young was an advantage at that time because of the physical requirements of Bart's care. In addition to school, Bart attended an Easter Seals camp each summer.

Bart's siblings are a brother, forty-three years old, and a sister, forty-five, who live out of state, as does their father. Katie said that the couple's divorce had nothing to do with Bart, but that other factors, including being very young when they married, would have led to a divorce, with or without a child with a disability. Katie felt that her other children were touched by Bart's disability and learned compassion, which she said was a positive in their lives.

Once Bart was out of school and on his own, he had some rocky times. He had a history of making poor dating choices. He was once married for ten days. Katie attributes some of Bart's current well-being to his now-retired caseworker at the Department of Rehabilitative Services (now DARS). Even though he and his caseworker often "butted heads," he kept close watch on Bart. It was through the caseworker that Katie learned of his present marriage. Somehow, Bart managed to travel to the bank in his wheelchair, and by using the name of his brother (who is on the account), he withdrew eighty dollars in order to get married.

Bart lives in an apartment with his wife of eight years, who has a form of dwarfism. Katie feels that his wife adds to Bart's stability and that the marriage is doing well. Bart has a daily aide, who Katie described as "wonderful." He previously went through a succession of less suitable aides (according to stories I have heard from others, this is not unusual). His wife has a job, but they have to be careful that her earnings remain within certain limits so that he doesn't lose benefits. Bart volunteers at a church answering the phone, the current job market for him being virtually nonexistent. Katie says that Bart is very good at using the phone to get information. He also uses a voice program for verbal word processing on his computer. He goes wherever he wants to, although Katie says she doesn't know how he's so successful getting around. He doesn't read Braille and cannot manage money, having no concept of its value. However, he did figure out how much money he needed to get married and how to get it.

When I asked if faith played a role in her parenting of Bart, Katie said that the source of her strength is her own personal stamina and drive. She said that in the past, she has gone to bed and cried, feeling that she "had not been a good mom" if the day didn't go particularly well. She never thought of not taking care of Bart and his siblings. She has a strong belief system and, although she was raised Catholic, does not have a church at present. Her family and friends are her supports, as is her current husband of fifteen years.

At this point, she is comfortable with the provisions for Bart's future. She set up a special needs trust and feels that with his wife and his siblings, he'll be fine when she's no longer around. In closing, Katie mentioned how she wished she could "wave the magic wand" to make things change, adding that Bart had taught her a lot. We ended our visit with a discussion about the changes in perception of people with disabilities today as opposed to when our children were young; we both felt that things are more positive now.

## Broader Acceptance of People with Disabilities

Children and adults with disabilities are more visible and accepted today. When I travel with Chris, people are kind towards him. They seem to understand if he gets a bit impatient and speaks out. I am asked no questions when I request early boarding on a flight. On one occasion, we were eating lunch at the Atlanta airport before flying home, and for some reason, Chris threw up. Immediately, strangers came to our table, bringing a lot of paper napkins and asking if he was okay (he was).

As I thought about writing this book, I started to collect newspaper articles about people with disabilities from our local paper, the *Virginian-Pilot*. A feature in a newspaper means that some reporter and editor think that the person and their story are newsworthy. I don't remember seeing many articles featuring people with disabilities in the newspaper during my school years. In four years of college, the only printed word on the subject I remember was a text for my class on exceptional children.

Over the past eighteen months, I have clipped many stories about children and adults from our local paper. The stories cover a wide range of issues, from a woman with disabilities who needed a backyard pool so she could exercise to a story about a private school for children with autism. In addition, these stories were run:

- Medicaid waivers for housing and the eleven thousand people in Virginia on a waiting list for a residential waiver
- a high school student with hearing loss who received a special stethoscope to help her pursue a career as a nurse
- a couple reaching out to parents of children with Down syndrome
- a ninth-grader who participates in indoor soccer in his wheelchair during PE
- a man with ALS who received a college degree using only his eyes on his computer
- a thirty-nine-year-old woman and her parents, focusing on their coaching her in Special Olympics speed skating
- the benefits and challenges in employing people who have autism
- a front page story about my son, Chris, and the change in the prevocational Medicaid waiver program, causing him to lose his (less-than-minimum-wage) piecework job
- a follow-up story several months later about Chris's new placement.

Because of social media, stories travel quickly. I posted the first article about Chris on Facebook, and others reposted it. Someone saw the story in a New Orleans newspaper a few weeks later. Many people ask me about what is happening with his work situation now and want to know how he's doing with the changeover to day support. I'm happy to report that he's enjoying his new placement, which is a combination of day support and work. The reporter who wrote the story, Elizabeth Simpson, told me that she's had comments from readers all over the country about the article.

The good news is that awareness of children and adults with disabilities is far greater than it was in the past. Also, the compassion factor seems to be growing and the shame factor declining. In earlier times, Rosemary Kennedy's family kept her hidden from the public, and her father gave approval for a lobotomy operation without consulting his wife or any other family member. President Franklin D. Roosevelt would always be photographed sitting at a desk or standing behind a podium to hide his braces. It was not until his monument was erected in Washington DC that he was depicted in his wheelchair. To demonstrate how far public opinion has changed, Governor Greg Abbott of Texas was seen in his wheelchair every day throughout the coverage of 2017's Hurricane Harvey, and his disability was never mentioned in the news.

# Questions for Group Discussion or Self-Reflection

1. How does the parent of an adult who chooses to be independent walk the fine line between being concerned and being intrusive?

_____

_____

_____

_____

_____

_____

_____

2. Could you let Bart make his own choices? What would be most difficult?

_____

_____

_____

_____

_____

_____

_____

3. How do parents decide whether to follow a doctor's advice to place their child out of the home?

_____

_____

_____

_____

_____

_____

_____

_____

4. When might an out-of-home placement be the best solution for both the family and the child?

_____

_____

_____

_____

_____

_____

_____

## Planning for the Future

We parents would like to provide a safe and sound future for our adult children with disabilities, as much as possible. Counting on siblings to be providers when we are no longer around raises many questions. Where will the siblings be living? What will their particular situation be when needed to assist a sibling with a disability? Who will be best able to care for the brother or sister with special needs? What services will be available where the siblings live? Will government regulations be the same? Will federal and state funding remain the same? We plan as best we can for children and hope and pray that it will be appropriate and adequate. All we want as parents is to have our adult children with special needs be healthy, happy, and loved. But sometimes, the future seems like an unsolvable puzzle.

Peggy Lou Morgan's book *Parenting an Adult with Disabilities or Special Needs: Everything You Need to Know to Plan for and Protect Your Child's Future* attempts to cover all the areas that concern every parent. Morgan discusses both adults with special needs who moved out of their homes after their public education ended and those who remained in the home. She writes, "If we wait for services to become available because we are aged or unable to care for our adult children, we will not have the same ability to aid in the transition. The longer an adult child remains in the nest, the more difficult will be her transition to an adult situation."(1)

In chapter 6, I related my discussion with Paul regarding the traumatic situation for adults with special needs when the remaining parent dies and they have to be moved to an unfamiliar situation, often a group home where they don't know anyone. Imagine yourself as that person who suddenly is forced to leave your home and what's familiar to you. How would it feel to begin in a totally new place where you know no one, while grieving your loss, which you may not fully understand?

People can become depressed, get angry, and have acting-out behaviors as their only way of expressing their feelings. In an episode of the PBS television series *Call the Midwife*, set in 1950s-1960s London, a young man named Reggie with Down syndrome was in this distressing situation. He lived with his mother, who died suddenly. She had trained him to watch the clock face to know when she was coming home. One day, she didn't return from work, and Reggie sat at the kitchen table for hours, watching the clock. His cousin John and his wife, a couple in their sixties, learned of the death and came to get Reggie. They decided to bring him to their home. It didn't work out as planned. They both had day jobs, and because Reggie was unfamiliar with their house, some mishaps ensued. He locked himself out when he picked up a delivered parcel outside the front door. On another day, he left the gas burners on when he unsuccessfully tried to light the stove. After that, John brought him to work every day, part of which was gardening. Reggie liked the arrangement, but the couple was getting worn out from care. They looked into the local institution for people with intellectual disabilities, but that was grim and not an option they would consider. They eventually found a kinder, gentler place where people were treated well and Reggie could have a true home. John and his wife were reluctant to send Reggie away but felt they had to. Subsequent visits reassured them that Reggie was doing well and enjoying his gardening work.

Reggie's mother thought that she was doing the right thing by caring for Reggie all her life. She had trained him well to function in the home with a strict regimen. But without his mother, Reggie was suddenly, totally lost, not even able to quite comprehend what death meant. Through caring family and friends, he eventually understood, however, and now enjoys his new home.

In 2012, Roger, my husband, Chris's stepfather, died. I told Chris that Roger was now in heaven. For almost three years, every time I was with

Chris, he would ask, "Where is Roger?" and my reply would be, "Heaven." The conversation would go back and forth for a few rounds, with a slight variation of that wording, until Chris was satisfied for that day. Even though he visited Roger in the hospital and had been at the memorial service, it took him a long time to put the illness and death all together so that it was solid in his mind. Having those ongoing conversations was difficult for me, as I felt the grief and pain each time we went through the ritual, but I couldn't let him know how painful it was. Now, we visit the columbarium in the church where Roger's ashes are placed. We read the plaque and remember Roger together, and the questions have stopped. I wonder how Chris will react when I die, but I have to leave that in his brothers' and other caregivers' hands.

I take comfort in knowing that Chris is in a solid living situation and that no upsetting, sudden moves would have to be made for him if I'm no longer around. I also know that if things change somehow, his brothers will come together to make the best decision. We've discussed several possibilities, using different scenarios. I keep his brothers in the loop on all events of his life and on all regulation changes, so that they are current. I have one file drawer in my home that has all of Chris's information and documents so that anyone could easily access whatever they needed.

Parents should consider creating a caregiver training manual, as discussed in Morgan's book. Topics would include the person's personality, likes and dislikes, the best means of communication, preferences for room arrangement, elements that might trigger acting-out behaviors (such as bright lights or loud noises), and health, diet, and safety protocols. Parents can, of course, add any other sections they see as important, such as preferences for worship in a faith community.

Morgan also advises creating a storybook of pictures and family history for the person to take wherever they go. This is not only a remembrance album, it could provide insight for caregivers about connections to family and friends, demonstrating that this person doesn't exist in isolation. I've discussed with my sons having "eyes on the ground" when I'm no longer able to oversee Chris. People who are in care receive better treatment when it is known that someone, friends or family, will be visiting on a regular basis. Some places have a higher turnover of staff than others, but the person in care also needs to keep those familiar connections for a sense of belonging and still being part of a family.

The first genetic testing my son Chris had was for Down syndrome. He's had subsequent genetic testing over the years, but all we found were false conclusions and ruling out of many conditions so far. He recently had Whole Exome Screening, which looked at twenty thousand of his genes. The results were that they found a mutation in one specific gene that could be responsible for his intellectual disability. This result has been found in only a few people; the doctor sent me a journal article on a child with this same mutation. The physical description of the boy sounded exactly like Chris. For now, the only action available was to consent to have the results put into the database for further research, but we now know that his brothers and nieces and nephews cannot pass this disability on, as the mutation is original to Chris.

If you are a parent who does not have a name or cause for your child's disability, I urge you to continue to ask for further testing. There are genetics labs connected to children's hospitals all over the country, and if your child is an adult, you can get a referral for an adult screening. Genetic technology continues to expand exponentially. The costs keep coming down; in many cases, insurance companies are covering the cost of the tests, and other help may be available.

# Questions for Group Discussion or Self-Reflection

1. In the past, we didn't think about retirement for people with Down syndrome, because their lifespan was not long. Now many people with disabilities are living long lives, with that population becoming gray-haired. What kind of programs and supports will be needed for people with disabilities in retirement age?

_____

_____

_____

_____

_____

_____

_____

_____

_____

_____

_____

_____

2. Is there a need for additional laws or regulations to support people with disabilities who are aging?

_____

_____

_____

_____

_____

_____

_____

_____

_____

_____

_____

_____

3. What are your concerns for your adult child with special needs as aging occurs?

_____

_____

_____

_____

_____

_____

_____

_____

_____

_____

_____

# REFERENCES AND RESOURCES

All scripture quotations are from the King James Version (KJV).

Chapter 1

1. R. S. Cook, *Parenting the Child with Special Needs*. Grand Rapids, Michigan: Zondervan, 1992.

2. X. Wei and J. W. Yu, "The concurrent and longitudinal effects of child disability types and health on family experiences," *The Journal of Maternal and Child Health,* 16, 2012, 100-108.

3. H. B. Waldman, S. P. Perlman, and M. Garey, "Will you and the life of your child with a disability be better after your divorce?" *The Exceptional Parent* (Online), 45:8, 2015, 16-18.

4. A. F. Farrell, G. L. Bowen and D. C. Swick, "Network supports and resiliency among U.S. military spouses with children with special care health needs," *Family Relations,* 2014, 63, 55-70.

Chapter 2

1. The SIS was developed by the American Association on Intellectual and Developmental Disabilities (www.aaidd.org).

2. Medicaid and Home- and Community-Based services: https://www.medicaid.gov/medicaid/hcbs/index.html

3. Each state has its own name for a department that provides rehabilitation, disability, and aging services. The Virginia Department of Aging and Rehabilitative Services (rsa.ed.gov/) is a state program, in conjunction with the federal Office of Rehabilitation, which is under the US Department of Education.

4. https://arcminnesota.org/organizer/research-and-training-center-on-comminity-living/

5. L'Arche: https://www.larcheusa.org/

Chapter 4

1. *Altercasting* is a theory developed by E. Weinstein and P. Deutschber (http://changingminds.org/techniques/general/more_methods/altercasting.htm).

2. Overseas adoptions: https://travel.state.gov/content/adoptionsabroad/en/adoption-process.htm

3. T. Bell, "Adopting the international child with special needs," 2006. http://www.rainbowkids.com/adoption-stories/adopting-the-international-child-with-special-needs-206

Chapter 5

1. The National Down Syndrome Society (http://www.ndss.org/Down-Syndrome/What-Is-Down-Syndrome/)

2. ABLE National Resource Center (http://ablenrc.org)

Chapter 6

1. Disabled Military Child Protection Act (http://www.specialneedsalliance.org/the-voice/disabled-military-child-protection-act/)

2. Military One Source: (800) 342-9647. A special needs consultant is available.

## Chapter 7

1. Dandy-Walker malformation (https://ghr.nlm.nih.gov/condition/dandy-walker-malformation)

2. The Individuals with Disabilities Education Improvement Act (http://idea.ed.gov)

3. References for microboards:

*Australia.* The bright, inviting site offers a number of resources that would be helpful to anyone forming a personal or statewide microboard association (http://microboard.org.au/).

M. Forster. A step-by-step "how-to" for microboards; refers to processes in Georgia (http://www.bellaonline.com/articles/art170777.asp)

Georgia: An overview of the microboard process in Georgia but also general information applicable to all (http://www.gamicroboards.org/index.html).

J. Golden. "Self-directed support corporations (SDSC) and microboards. What a difference a SDSC can make: Joshua's house incorporated!" (http://www.bridges4kids.org/pdf/Golden-Microboards.pdf)

Iowa: Extensive information for Iowa and elsewhere. Useful information for anyone interested in a microboard. http://www.iowacompass.org/microboards.htm

Tennessee Association of Microboards and Human Services Co-ops (https://tn.gov/cdd/article/microboards-and-human-service-co-ops)

Texas: A clear, concise PowerPoint presentation of the first microboard in Texas (http://www.twogetherconsulting.com/wp-content/uploads/Texas'-First-Microboard-handout.pdf)

John Shea. California, United Kingdom, and British Columbia microboards. Resources that are both directly related to microboards as well as a wealth of other resources for persons with disabilities (http://www.dimagine.com/page20.html).

David and Faye Wetherow. Microboards and microboard association design, development and implementation. They created the first microboard in Manitoba, Canada, in 1984 (http://www.communityworks.info/articles/microboard.htm)

The Wisconsin Association of Microboards is under construction as of this writing but lists contact information (http://wisconsinmicroboards.com/Wisconsin_Microboards_Association/Welcome.html).

The Virginia Microboard Association (http://virginiamicroboards.org/microboards/)

4.  Christine Towers, "Thinking ahead: Improving support for people with learning disabilities and their families to plan for the future," *Foundation for people with learning disabilities.* London, 2013, http://www. Learningdisabilities.org.uk.

## Chapter 8

1.  K. F. Jackson, *Loving Samantha.* Virginia Beach, VA: Kohler Studios, 2014.

2.  The American Association for Intellectual and Developmental Disabilities (https://aaidd.org)

3.  The Faith Inclusion Network of Hampton Roads (www.faithinclusionnetwork.org)

4.  J. Philo, *The Caregiver's Notebook. An Organizational Tool and Support to Help You Care for Others,* Grand Rapids, Michigan: Discovery House, 2014.

5.  J. Philo, *Different Dream Parenting: A Practical Guide to Raising a Child with Special Needs.* Grand Rapids, Michigan: Discovery House, 2011.

6.  E. Colson, *Dancing with Max. A mother and son who broke free.* Grand Rapids, Michigan: Zondervan, 2010. (Prologue and epilogue by Emily's father, Chuck Colson; http://www.emilycolson.com)

Chapter 9

1.  Turner syndrome information: http://www.mayoclinic. org/diseases-conditions/turner-syndrome/basics/definition/ CON-20032572

2.  https://ghr.nlm.nih.gov/condition/turner-syndrome#genes

3.  Autism information: https://www.cellmedicine.com/ autism-and-stem-cell-publications/

4.  See chapter 2, note 3.

5.  J. E. H. Barnett and R. Crippen, "Eight steps to school-based employment training for adolescents with autism spectrum disorder and intellectual disability," *Physical Disabilities: Education and Related Services,* 33(2), 2014, 1-15. doi: 10.14434/pders.v33i2.5186

6.  See chapter 5, note 3.

7.  *Young Life* is a nonprofit, nondenominational organization reaching out to young people in all fifty states and around the world. According to their website (http://www.younglife.org), "Young Life began with a few simple ideas about sharing the truth of God's love with adolescents. Seven decades later, those simple ideas have become time-tested methods for reaching out to middle school, high school, and college students in friendship and in hope."

8.  S. Ayers, "Pity the parents of special needs children: Effects & coping," *Psychology Today,* 2013 (https://www. psychologytoday.com/blog/insight-is-2020/201310/ pity-the-parents-special-needs-children-effects-coping).

9. Sima Ash, "Working moms of special needs children: Tips for balancing life with a special needs child" (https://www.thebalance.com/working-moms-of-special-needs-children-3515737).

Chapter 10

1. Leigh's disorder information: Genetic and Rare Disease Information Center (GARD), part of the National Institutes of Health (NIH), https://rarediseases.info.nih.gov/diseases/6877/leighs-disease

2. https://inclusioninnovations.com

3. http://www.Chabad.org/inclusion is the official website for the worldwide Chabad-Lubavitch movement.

4. Organizations that promote inclusion of people with disabilities in Jewish congregations:

   • Shabbaton: http://jewishtimes.com/63353/jewish-deafblind-adults-share-faith-community-at-shabbaton-2017/news/
   • The Disabilities Inclusion Learning Center: http://www.disabilitiesinclusion.org
   • YACHAD: http://www.Yachad.org

Chapter 11

1. P. Harris, *One Day at a Time*, Harrisonburg, Virginia: ParkView Press, 1979.

2. Organizations that support parents who have adult children with disabilities:

   The ARC (http://www.thearc.org/) is the former Association for Retarded Children. Its current focus is on people with intellectual and developmental disabilities and their families, caregiver, and advocates in all aspects of life. It has state and local chapters, and an annual conference open to the public.

Special Olympics, founded in 1968 by Eunice Kennedy Shriver (sister of the late President John F. Kennedy), serves individuals of all ages who have intellectual disabilities. Athletes learn, enjoy, and compete in a variety of sports on many levels. No one is ever charged a fee to participate (http://www.specialolympics.org/Sections/Who_We_Are/About_Intellectual_Disabilities.aspx).

## Chapter 13

1. Duchenne's Muscular Dystrophy (https://www.mda.org/disease/duchenne-muscular-dystrophy)

2. Post-secondary accommodations for students: American Psychology Association website (http://www.apa.org/pi/disability/dart/toolkit-three.aspx)

3. "Rights of students with disabilities in higher education: A guide for college and university students," Disability Rights California, Protection & Advocacy System (http://www.disabilityrightsca.org/pubs/530901.pdf).

## Chapter 14

1. P. L. Morgan, *Parenting an Adult with Disabilities or Special Needs. Everything You Need to Know to Plan for and Protect Your Child's Future,* New York: AMACOM Books, 2009.

## Chapter 15

Resources for Future Planning

1. The ARC: https://futureplanning.thearc.org/pages/learn/future-planning-101

The following is from their website:

> Future Planning is creating a guide for a person with an intellectual or developmental disability (I/DD) to lead a good life as independently as possible. A plan is important throughout all stages of life and especially in the future after the parent or caregiver is no longer able to provide support.
>
> A person-centered future plan should reflect the wishes of the person with I/DD, as well as his or her parents, siblings, extended family members and friends, and other important people in his or her life. The plan should include information about all aspects of a person's life including:
>
> o   Daily routines, needs and supports
> o   Living arrangements
> o   Finances, including the family and person's public benefits, assets, incomes, trusts, insurance policies
> o   Doctors' contact information and information about the person's medical history (including any medications and food allergies)
> o   Decision-making support
> o   Education history
> o   Details about the person's employment, leisure activities, religious beliefs, behaviors, interests, friendships, and other important relationships.

2.   The Sibling and Leadership Network: Siblingleadership.org

> From their website: "The mission of the Sibling Leadership Network is to provide siblings of individuals with disabilities the information, support and tools to advocate with their brothers and sisters and to promote the issues important to them and their entire families."

3.   Charting the Life Course

> http://www.lifecoursetools.com/charting-the-life-course-guide/

From their website:

Charting the Life Course is a framework that was developed to help individuals with disabilities and families at any age or stage of life think about what they need to know, identify how to find or develop supports, and discover what it takes to live the lives they want to live. Individuals and families may focus on their current situation and stage of life but may also find it helpful to look ahead to start thinking about what they can do or learn now that that will help build an inclusive productive life in the future."

4. Think College (https://thinkcollege.net) is a website that lists programs in the United States for persons with intellectual and developmental disabilities desiring a college experience. The website is searchable by state. Anyone interested in attending a college should call the institution and verify where programs are located, as websites may not always be up to date.

Printed in the United States
By Bookmasters